# A Casebook for
# SECOND LANGUAGE
# TEACHER EDUCATION

## Reflecting on the Language Classroom

Amy B. Gooden

and Maria N. Zlateva

D1609162

UNIVERSITY OF MICHIGAN

ANN ARBOR

ISBN-13: 978-0-472-03703-2 (print)
ISBN-13: 978-0-472-12456-5 (ebook)

2021    2020    2019    2018                    4        3        2        1

# Acknowledgments

This book is the result of decades of teaching thousands of students and student teachers. We owe them insights, inspiration, and knowledge.

The casebook would not have been possible without the contributions of many colleagues over the years—at Harvard University, Boston University, and Lesley University. The cases included here evolved in each of these contexts through numerous conversations, pilots, and classroom experiences. We are grateful for those enriching interactions.

We also appreciate Kelly Sippell's editorial help in shaping the book for a broader audience.

Finally, our deepest gratitude goes to our families: We could not have completed this project without their support and love.

—Amy Gooden and Maria Zlateva

# Contents

# Introduction

The 21st century's multicultural and multilingual world has spurred the need for competent second language (L2) teachers in a range of K–12 and post-secondary contexts. L2 teachers have the immense responsibility of equipping future global citizens with the gift of communication in another language so they can voice their needs and ideas across linguistic and cultural boundaries.

**Case-based pedagogy** is an innovative sociocultural approach to second language teacher education, sometimes referred to as **SLTE** (pronounced like "slate"), that forces participants to grapple with exactly the kinds of dilemmas and decisions teachers confront every day. In doing so, it redefines the traditional educational dynamic in which the professor dispenses knowledge and students passively receive it. One key characteristic of case-based pedagogy is the case method, a teaching approach that consists of presenting students with a case that puts them in the role of a decision-maker facing a problem. In a case method classroom, the instructor and students are actively engaged in dissecting the information in order to explore the context, characters, issues, options, criteria, and solutions (Ellet, 2007).

With more than two decades of experience teaching language using the case-based method at Harvard University, we have productively continued to apply this approach in these settings:

- pre-service undergraduate and graduate ESL/TESOL/Bilingual K–12 teacher licensure programs
- pre-service undergraduate and graduate Modern Foreign Language and World Language K–12 licensure programs
- in-service professional development workshops with teachers across content areas who are interested in supporting the language needs of diverse learners
- in-service professional development workshops for those in Modern Foreign Language and World Language departments
- graduate TESOL education programs
- in-house faculty development in English for Academic Purposes (EAP) and intensive English programs (IEPs)

This *Casebook* offers written representations of actual language classroom dilemmas from private, charter, and public schools in urban and suburban contexts. It also offers a range of language program designs at elementary, secondary, and tertiary levels: K–12 English as a second language (ESL)/bilingual education/sheltered English immersion (SEI); modern foreign language (MFL); and post-secondary EAP contexts.

This innovative casebook can be used successfully as a stand-alone text in the typical courses in language teacher preparation programs in schools of education, such as:

- Practicum or Student Teaching Seminars
- Methods of Teaching Modern Foreign Language, TESOL, and Bilingual Education courses
- Issues in Bilingualism
- Language and Literacy
- Sociolinguistics and Education
- Applied Linguistics
- ESL and SEI Endorsement
- Intercultural/Multicultural Education

The book can also be used as a supplementary text in any of these courses and as a resource in professional development programs for in-service language teachers in K–12 and post-secondary contexts.

Language teacher educators can use this text in their courses and workshops to build on and extend theoretical foundations, while making critical practical connections. All the cases are based on real-life dilemmas faced by practitioners in the field and have been informed by discussions with pre-service and in-service student teachers.

The 12 cases presented here cover a range of issues that practitioners are likely to face in their respective teaching contexts. All the cases deal with hot topics and trending issues that will resonate with readers. Most of the cases reflect authentic situations in K–12 language teaching, while a smaller number of post-secondary cases address key aspects of teaching academic English in the global higher education context. A primary criterion for selecting which cases would be included was alignment with national and state subject matter knowledge standards for language teachers. Although all the names of schools and individuals are pseudonyms, in some of the cases, readers will notice references to specific state and local regulations and policies. However, based on our teaching of this material, we are confident that the issues presented are generalizable.

The cases are accompanied by pre- and post-problem sets and in-class discussion questions. Each case is designed to promote specific language learning and teaching goals. Broadly defined, learning with cases involves an instructional and curricular blend of individual reflection and group analysis of authentic cases.

## A Few Important Notes

One thing we would like to state up front: In some situations, readers may detect stereotypical thinking about culture, race, ethnicity, and socioeconomic conditions in the case apparatus. This is a conscious choice because our experience with case discussions shows that including such perspectives and attitudes **generates critical analysis of the real issues in contemporary multicultural and multilingual contexts.** In the same vein, rather than fueling stereotypes, the provocative—and sometimes extreme—language is **intended to hone readers' sensitivity to and awareness of the cross-cultural dimension of language teaching.**

In the spirit of the Harvard Business School case structure, the cases included are **not intended as exemplars of practice to be emulated or illustrations of existing theories;** instead, they are **problem-based narratives** that resist clear-cut answers or solutions and remain open-ended in order to stimulate further investigation and reflection. The narrative style is **purposefully neutral** and, at times, deliberately includes seemingly irrelevant information or redundant details, there to serve as distractors from the core issues. The goal is to **mimic the complexity of the classroom** where teachers confront a range of pedagogical and learning challenges, and the ensuing experience is one of being steeped like a teabag in a hot cup of reality where critical, real-time decisions depend on keen professional discernment.

Even though the use of the case method does not presuppose familiarity with key theoretical underpinnings in linguistics or second language education methods, we would encourage participants with limited formative training in these subjects to consult the recommended readings that accompany the online Commentary before reading each case. This will ensure richer and more informed discussion and analysis of the issues in the case.

The Commentary (available online) for each case outlines the specific objectives of each case and is designed to assist professors, professional development leaders, and anyone who teaches with the *Casebook*. The Commentary features:

- additional background information for the case
- overarching implications of the case in terms of teacher knowledge, praxis, and thinking
- specified language teaching and learning outcomes
- suggestions for best-practice instruction

## Overall Structure of the Book

The case chapters are organized as follows:

> Chapter 2 includes Elementary ESL/SEI/Bilingual Education cases with accompanying discussion questions and problem sets.
>
> Chapter 3 covers Secondary ESL/SEI/TESOL cases with accompanying discussion questions and problem sets.
>
> Chapter 4 includes Secondary Modern Foreign Language cases with accompanying discussion questions and problem sets.
>
> Chapter 5 presents Post-Secondary English for Academic Purposes cases with accompanying discussion questions and problem sets.

Table I.1 charts the primary pedagogical issues of each case for quick reference and to allow users to find a synthesis of the issues and objectives by case or setting.

**Table I.1**

Chart of Cases and Pedagogies

| Case | Language Teaching Objectives | Other SLTE Objectives |
|---|---|---|
| **Stoney Hill** | • Weave language and content objectives and shelter ESL instruction across content areas<br>• Meet rigorous content standards<br>• Make content meaningful, engaging, and relevant to learners to promote engagement<br>• Establish home-school connections to reinforce learning | • Stimulate curricular creativity in high-stakes testing environments<br>• Manage a multilevel classroom<br>• Embrace problem-solving orientations, including all stakeholders |
| **Dean School** | • Support students' literacy development<br>• Integrate the four domains of language<br>• Build learner background knowledge<br>• Design varied and differentiated tasks<br>• Use appropriate supplementary materials<br>• Design effective lessons | • Develop culturally responsive curriculum |
| **Hanlen School** | • Develop English learner support for emerging bilinguals/newcomers<br>• Teach tiered vocabulary<br>• Incorporate ongoing formative assessments | • Cultivate relationships with students' families<br>• Involve all specialists to distinguish between language and cognitive needs |
| **Reddington High** | • Use best practices to promote reading comprehension<br>• Connect reading and writing tasks<br>• Differentiate instruction for varying reading proficiency levels | • Hone sensitivity to the sociocultural worlds and needs of multicultural, multilingual learners |

**Table I.1 (continued)**

Chart of Cases and Pedagogies

| Case | Language Teaching Objectives | Other SLTE Objectives |
|---|---|---|
| John Cassidy High | ▪ Contextualize grammar and vocabulary instruction<br>▪ Scaffold learning to make content accessible<br>▪ Encourage cooperative learning<br>▪ Adopt research-based approaches to vocabulary instruction | ▪ Create a welcoming and inclusive learning environment<br>▪ Encourage teacher motivation and collaboration |
| Rose Hall High | ▪ Promote extrinsic and intrinsic motivation<br>▪ Contextualize language instruction<br>▪ Design task-based/project-based language lessons and follow up<br>▪ Encourage broad-based participation | ▪ Consider the impact of sociocultural factors on academic success |
| Oxford High | ▪ Conform to ACTFL standards<br>▪ Contextualize grammar instruction<br>▪ Employ task-based and communicative approaches to language teaching<br>▪ Set rigorous standards for all students | ▪ Avoid teacher burnout<br>▪ Encourage professional development<br>▪ Capitalize on teacher aids |
| Charles Watson High | ▪ Promote listening comprehension skills and sequence tasks productively<br>▪ Use technology effectively<br>▪ Incorporate authentic materials<br>▪ Bridge listening to speaking activities | ▪ Develop higher-order thinking skills<br>▪ Vary instruction, content, and format |

**Table I.1 (continued)**

Chart of Cases and Pedagogies

| Case | Language Teaching Objectives | Other SLTE Objectives |
|---|---|---|
| Decartes Immersion School | ▪ Teach in a language immersion model<br>▪ Respond to the needs of heritage language learners<br>▪ Develop a differentiated, multicultural curriculum<br>▪ Scaffold speaking tasks<br>▪ Lower the learners' affective filter | ▪ Consider theories of acculturation<br>▪ Engage in reflective practice |
| Morell Community College | ▪ Design explicit lesson plans, with clear purpose, goals, and tasks<br>▪ Provide scaffolding for the language component in an EAP context<br>▪ Balance receptive and productive skills<br>▪ Develop formative and summative assessment strategies | ▪ Cultivate cross-cultural sensitivity among students<br>▪ Develop student autonomy and agency |
| Greenview University | ▪ Teach both disciplinary and linguistic knowledge<br>▪ Demystify and promote academic integrity<br>▪ Model and monitor the writing process<br>▪ Assess style in writing | ▪ Clarify cultural notions of academic success<br>▪ Coordinate institutional goals and policies |
| Lakeborough College | ▪ Build academic literacies<br>▪ Practice critical thinking and analysis<br>▪ Model academic discourse moves<br>▪ Distinguish among subject, procedural, content, and language knowledge<br>▪ Select objective-driven teaching materials | ▪ Extend teaching beyond the classroom<br>▪ Negotiate students' varied positions and opinions<br>▪ Encourage metalinguistic awareness |

# Chapter 1

# Case-Based Pedagogy and a Guide to Learning through Cases

For the past 25 years, the field of second language teacher education (SLTE) has wrestled with the question of how best to prepare future educators and has gradually shifted to sociocultural approaches. Vigorous professional debate has highlighted these issues in SLTE programs:

- a neglect for the sociocultural view of teaching and learning and an overemphasis on the teacher-centered, lecture-based model
- a need for critical reflection, rarely including the student teacher experiences into the curriculum
- a lack of a bridge between theory and practice
- poor modeling of critical thinking strategies and learning processes (Freeman and Johnson, 2005; Hedgcock, 2002; Johnson, 2006; Richards, 2008; Smith, 2005; Tedick, 2005)

Two central aspects of L2 teacher preparation—knowledge base and pedagogy—have undergone scrutiny recently. The knowledge base has been re-examined to question the traditional language-based disciplines (linguistics and second language acquisition) as the core curriculum for SLTE (Freeman, 2002; Johnson & Golombek, 2011); there is now a call to incorporate learners' experiences and provide opportunities for reflective practice. Moreover, in a radical departure from the long-held rationalist view of teaching as transfer of knowledge, a sociocultural shift in traditional pedagogy urges SLTE programs to create conditions for the co-construction of knowledge and understanding through social participation.

The current field of second language education is contextually diverse: It is concerned with the preparation of knowledgeable and skilled English as a second language, English as a foreign language, bilingual education, modern foreign language, and language immersion educators in national and international PreK–12 and post-secondary contexts. In the past, research in second language education was sometimes fragmented, and the field has only recently attempted to pull together all of its resources to gain a better understanding of second language teacher education and the issues facing the profession. In the process, case-based pedagogy, which utilized both cases and the case method, has emerged as a particularly innovative instructional approach.

The core concepts of case-based pedagogy are reminiscent of Greek and Chinese philosophers of thought. It is a well-established pedagogy in schools of business, law, medicine, and social work. The research that does exist in teacher education programs employing the case method indicates that it successfully develops various types of teacher knowledge, teacher thinking, and self-efficacy (Moje & Wade, 1997; Shulman, 1992) and serves as modeling of good practice (Kaste, 2003). The results of two existing SLTE studies (Haley, 2008; Reichelt, 2000) that incorporated cases and case discussions point to the power of this method to address specific pedagogical needs in the field:

- understanding the practice of standards
- linking theoretical perspectives to practice
- differentiating instruction for diversity

## The Case Method: Overview

The concepts of case and the case method are firmly defined in the fields of business, law, and medicine. Christensen and Hansen (1987) offer a clear definition from a business perspective:

> A case is a partial, historical, clinical study of a situation which has confronted a practicing administrator or managerial group. Presented in narrative form to encourage student involvement, it provides data—substantive and process—essential to an analysis of a specific situation, for the framing of alternative action programs, and for their implementation recognizing the complexity and ambiguity of the practical world. (p. 27)

The literature in teacher education, however, consists of multiple definitions, terminologies, and intended purposes. Essentially, it considers case a narrative representation of a real situation that places the reader(s) in the role of a participant in the situation. As Merseth (1996) notes:

> One common definition suggests that a case is a descriptive research document, often presented in narrative form that is based on a real-life situation or event. It attempts to convey a balanced, multidimensional representation of the context, participants, and reality of the situation. Cases are created explicitly for discussion and seek to include sufficient detail and information to elicit active analysis and interpretation by users with differing perspectives. (p. 722)

Case-based pedagogy is a means of developing teacher thinking, attitudes, and beliefs about issues in the field. Language teachers practicing it are not passive recipients of theories, principles, and strategies. Educators actively endeavor to accomplish goals they think to be important to their work (Clark & Peterson, 1986), and case studies give teachers the opportunity to reflect on their reasoning while at the same time providing an instrument that stimulates novel ways of thinking about decision-making and problem-solving.

Three key aspects of a case discussion are: (1) entering into a dialogical interaction with the self and others, (2) critical reflection, and (3) collaboration in a community of learning (Kleinfield, 1992). Users of this method first place themselves in the role of decision-maker as they read the situation and identify the problem. The next step is to perform the necessary analysis—examining the causes and considering alternative courses of actions to determine a set of recommendations.

Specifically, the case studies with accompanying problem sets are designed to help practitioners develop language teacher knowledge, thinking, and praxis. The in-class discussions and problem sets encourage language educators who learn via this approach to make connections to their own practice.

During the case discussion process, participants learn how to analyze complex problems and perform the necessary research to confront authentic problems or test their proposed solutions. They probe the issues at stake and are compelled to exercise evidence-based judgment in the dynamic process of exchanging perspectives and opinions. Faced with constraints that would be present in the real world, they have to suggest a course of action, which trains them to assume responsibility. Participants are expected to read all the case materials in advance and consult and collaborate with their peers in small groups before engaging with the entire class. They provide effective feedback on alternative courses so that, in the end, they have a set of recommendations.

# Case Methodology

The case chapters open with a narrative that presents an authentic pedagogical dilemma in a specific educational context. In line with traditional case study structure, the narrative of the real-life situation is supplemented with what are referred to as **exhibits,** which provide additional information and evidentiary basis for the discussion of the case. The exhibits are various artifacts (e.g., policy documents, school demographic data and statistics, state and national teaching standards, and lesson plans and curricula) "curated" to reflect the sociocultural dimension of case studies, which heavily influences current SLTE pedagogy. The framework for the case study consists of these stages:

1. Pre-case problem sets that ask participants to:
   a. **Chart** the issues
   b. **Write** a discussion decision response paper

2. In-class discussion through questions that cover these elements:
   a. **Big-picture analysis** to describe the context of the case
   b. **Stakeholders**—a description of the key participants and their perspectives
   c. **Surface issues**—problems that would be easy to identify in the case narratives at the pre-discussion stage
   d. **Deep issues**—curricular and instructional challenges that a language educator would discover after theoretically informed analysis
   e. **Evidence-based solutions** that propose options for solving the cases with research-based strategies and pedagogical experience
   f. **Teacher thinking** prompts that engage educators in critical and reflective practice

3. Post-case problem sets that ask the participants to:
   a. **categorize** their learning in terms of teacher knowledge, thinking, and dispositions
   b. **list** the learning objectives and implications for pedagogy as way to move toward praxis
   c. **consider** and **reflect on** other educators' perspectives and solutions through a set of authentic quotes that come from previous readers of the cases
   d. **reflect on** connections between the case and previous and current teaching experience, as well as on key take-aways for future praxis, by developing an action plan and writing a short paper
   e. **discuss** the theoretical basis for behaviors and solutions and then continue to explore the issues presented by the case through suggested theoretical resources

Each is followed by these problem sets:

## 1. PRE-CASE DISCUSSION PROBLEMS SETS

Complete the chart after reading the case.

| | |
|---|---|
| Facts | |
| Opinions | |
| Assumptions | |
| Theories referred or connected to (if any) | |
| Ambiguous language | |
| Criteria you used in analyzing the case (e.g., emotional vs. rational) | |
| Emerging options | |

Write a pre-case discussion decision paper. Include these points:

    a. options for case resolution

    b. criteria (a rational decision should always be made with a set of criteria)

    c. analysis of options

    d. recommendation (of the best choice among the options)

    e. action plan

## II. Case Discussion Questions

Under the skillful guidance of the case facilitator, students are expected to provide answers to a variety of questions. They consult with their peers in small groups before engaging with the entire class and do most of the talking as the case unfolds.

### Big-Picture Analysis

Describe the context of the case.

### Stakeholders

In small groups, assume the role of one of the case stakeholders. Write a statement/dialogue expressing this person's or group's hypothetical feelings and perspectives. Be prepared to act out your roles to the large group.

### Surface Issues

What are the surface issues in this case? What is happening here from an untrained perspective? What underlying assumptions or beliefs feed into this perspective?

### Deep Issues

Discuss the real issues in the case. Try to categorize them in terms of language teaching curriculum and instruction.

### Evidence-Based Solutions

In groups, develop evidence-based solutions for each issue. Whenever possible, refer to a theory or principle of language learning and teaching to support your proposed solutions.

### Teacher Thinking

In what ways does this case influence and/or reinforce your beliefs and dispositions as a teacher? Consult the Further Resources section to help with theoretically informed solutions.

## III. POST-CASE PROBLEM SETS

### *Post-Case Analysis*

A. Categorize what you learned as:

- teacher knowledge and praxis (e.g., content knowledge, curricular knowledge, pedagogical content knowledge and application)
- teacher thinking (e.g., beliefs, problem-solving strategies, prioritizing objectives, values, professional ethics, attitudes)

B. List:

- learning objectives that you discovered in the case
- potential learning outcomes
- implications for your pedagogical practices

C. The post-case problem sets introduce reactions from various perspectives. These quotes are from others who have read the cases for educational and pedagogical purposes. Read all of the quotes and then choose two about which to write a short response (put the quotes at the top of each response). Use these questions as a guide:

- What is the message the speaker is trying to convey? If possible, also explain why you chose the quote.
- What examples can you think of that connect to the themes presented?
- Can you relate the quote to a class discussion or to something you have read or experienced?

Note: The quotes are composites based on observations by both experienced and inexperienced teachers and are included to illustrate genuine (therefore occasionally extreme) reactions of practitioners to classroom situations similar to the scenarios in the cases. Some quotes may reveal an insufficient knowledge base, while others serve to illuminate good teacher instincts. Some quotes are purposefully provocative in order to trigger debate and reveal unspoken prejudices and stereotypes (sometimes witnessed in teacher rooms or watercooler talk). Our experience shows that the value of such statements lies in helping teachers (1) to develop the ability to reflect on holistic aspects of their teaching and (2) to categorize their experiences in terms of teacher knowledge, thinking, and praxis.

D. Write a reflection describing a take-away from the case in terms of praxis. Make sure to develop an action plan to resolve the case. Consider these questions as guidelines:

- In what ways did the case discussion influence your thinking about the case?
- Did you change your original decision or did the discussion reaffirm your position?
- What points had you not considered prior to the case discussion?
- How might the information you gained from this case be applicable to your current instructional setting and/or future instructional settings?
- What did you learn?
- What are you inspired to learn more about?
- How did the themes discussed in class apply to your experience?

E. Discuss what theoretical basis there is for:

- the stakeholders' behavior in the case.
- the solutions you proposed.

### *Further Reading and Resources*

The further readings are intended to provide the theoretical underpinnings for the discussions and can be used either in preparation for the case (for students with less methodological training) or as an extension of learning after the discussion (for participants with solid formative training). They inform case solutions based on research and best practices.

## References and Additional Resources

Christensen, C.R., & Hansen, A.J. (1987). *Teaching and the case method.* Boston: Harvard Business School Press.

Clark, C. M., & Peterson, P. L. (1986) Teachers' thought processes. In M. C. Witrock (Ed.), *Handbook of research on teaching* (3rd ed., pp. 255–296). New York: Macmillan.

Ellet, W. (2007). *The case study handbook.* Boston: Harvard Business School Press.

Freeman, D., & Johnson, K. E. (1998). Reconceptualizing the knowledge-base of language teacher education. *TESOL Quarterly, 32*(3), 397–417.

Freeman, D. (2002) The hidden side of the work: Teacher knowledge and learning to teach. *Language Teaching, 35,* 1–3.

Freeman, D., & Johnson, K. (2005). Toward linking teacher knowledge and student learning. In D. Tedick (Ed.), *Second language teacher education* (pp. 73–95). Mahwah, NJ: Lawrence Erlbaum.

Haley, M. (2008). Implications of using case study instruction in a second/foreign language classroom. *Foreign Language Annals, 37*(2) 290–300.

Hedgcock, J. S. (2002). Toward a socioliterate approach to second language teacher education. *Modern Language Journal, 86*(3), 299–317.

Johnson, K. E. (2006). The sociocultural turn and its challenges for second language teacher education. *TESOL Quarterly, 40(1)*, 235–257.

Johnson, K.E. (2009). *Second language teacher education: A sociocultural perspective.* New York: Routledge.

Johnson, K. E., & Golombek, P. R. (Eds.). (2011) *Research on second language teacher education: A sociocultural perspective on professional development.* New York: Routledge.

Kaste, J. (2003). Scaffolding through cases: Diverse constructivist teaching in the literacy methods course. *Teacher and Teacher Education, 20,* 31–45.

Kleinfeld, J. (1992). Learning to think like a teacher: The study of cases. In J. H. Shulman (Ed.), *Case methods in teacher education* (pp. 33–49). New York: Teachers College Press.

Merseth, K. (1996). Cases and case methods in teacher education. In J. Sikula (Ed.), *Handbook of research on teacher education* (pp. 722–744). New York: Macmillan.

Moje, E. B., & Wade, S. E. (1997). What case discussions reveal about teacher thinking. *Teaching and Teacher Education, 13,* 691–712.

Reichelt, M. (2000). Case studies in L2 teacher education. *ELT Journal, 54*(4), 346–353.

Richards, J. (2008). Second language teacher education today. *RELC Journal, 39*(2), 158–176.

Shulman, L. (1986). Those who understand: Knowledge growth in teaching. *Educational Researcher, 15*(2), 4–14.

Shulman, L. S. (1992). Toward a pedagogy of cases. In J. Shulman (Ed.), *Case methods in teacher education* (pp. 1–30). New York: Teachers College Press.

Smith, L. (2005). The impact of action research on teacher collaboration and professional growth. In D.J. Tedick (Ed.), *Second language teacher education: International perspectives* (pp. 199–204). Mahwah, NJ: Lawrence Erlbaum.

Tarone, E., & Allwright, D. (2005). Language teacher-learning and student language-learning: Shaping the knowledge base. In D. J. Tedick (Ed.), *Second language teacher education: International perspectives* (pp. 5–23). Mahwah, NJ: Lawrence Erlbaum.

Tedick, D. (2005). *Second language teacher education.* Mahwah, NJ: Lawrence Erlbaum.

Wright, T. (2010). Second language teacher education: Review of recent research on practice. *Language Teaching, 43*(3), 259–296.

# Chapter 2

# Cases in Elementary Settings: ESL/SEI/Bilingual Education

The cases in this chapter raise a range of contemporary issues concerning the education of elementary English learners in a variety of educational contexts. The first case, *Stoney Hill*, shows an upper-elementary sheltered English immersion (SEI) classroom in a low-performing school district that is struggling to raise student performance on state-mandated literacy and math exams. The second case, *Dean School*, places the reader in the position of a teacher who feels the prescribed curriculum is disjointed and does not provide sufficient differentiated access to grade-level content across disciplines in a diverse, multilevel SEI classroom. The third case, *Hanlen School*, presents the conundrum of determining whether a bilingual learner in kindergarten is experiencing academic difficulties due to language acquisition or cognitive challenges.

This chapter is designed to offer an open-ended forum for discussing important educational issues such as:

- integrating content and language objectives
- sheltered English immersion lesson planning in elementary settings
- meeting the unique needs of newcomer immigrants
- balanced literacy approaches
- differentiating instruction for elementary English learners
- vocabulary-building techniques
- parental engagement
- distinguishing between language learning and special education needs
- assessment

# ■■■■■■■■■■■■■■■ CASE 2.1 ■■■■■■■■■■■■■■■

# Stoney Hill

Stoney Hill Elementary School is one of the three elementary schools in the district, located in a residential area. The building complex hosts all the elementary schools, and students range from first to fourth graders. Over the past 20 years, a nearby university has contributed to improving the teacher and school effectiveness by sending in well-trained teachers, providing resources, and renovating the school building.

Ms. Cleary's classroom is a Level 2 English immersion class with 12 fourth grade English Language Learners (ELLs). Most students in the class have been in the country for at least two or three years, and more than half of them will start mainstream middle school classes in September. There are five girls and seven boys in the class, and their first languages include Arabic, Portuguese, Spanish, and Swahili. Ms. Cleary's classroom is always lively: "They are so active and talkative that the number of students does not matter in how to manage the classroom. It's all about students' characters," she says. In terms of fluency levels, some students read 82 words per minute while others read only 40 words. According to Ms. Cleary, students were assessed at the beginning of the school year, and their reading fluency has improved. Most students are able to write a few sentences but with spelling, punctuation, and verb tense mistakes. Students seem to be involved in writing, except for one student who avoids writing during the workshop and tends to get distracted.

Classroom management has been challenging for Ms. Cleary, although she has been a classroom teacher for almost ten years. This class has been quite tough compared to other classes she has taught. She mentions that by the time November arrives, students become united and work as a group; they share things, and their good personalities come out. Usually by that time in the school year, she understands the students better; however, this year is different. Ms. Cleary is concerned about two issues related to classroom management: students' behavior during the transitions between content lessons and the social behavior of one of the students.

Throughout the day, transitions between content sessions are very distracting. Ms. Cleary sometimes sends only a couple of students at a time to their cubbies to take out math textbooks; however, many students have trouble getting ready without talking, pushing other students, and racing to sit on the rug. To avoid distraction, Ms. Cleary sometimes calls on students to model what they are supposed to be doing according to the instructions given before the transition: put some books away in their cubbies and take out others, and come back to the rug quietly. Although students model perfectly when they are told to do so, on some days, they cannot go through transitions as smoothly as they did before.

Discipline has been a challenge throughout the semester: Students talk, shout, and distract other classmates during these breaks. This has become such an issue that Ms. Cleary stopped taking students to go to the restroom in a line together as a class, because lining them up and walking across the hallway to the restroom was taking too long. Instead, she lets them go to the restroom during the lessons only after receiving permission from her.

Another concerning issue for Ms. Cleary, and a major factor in distraction during the transitions, is one of the student's social behavior. His name is Ahmed. He has already attended all other elementary schools in the complex, switching from one classroom to another because of his unacceptable behavior. Ms. Cleary's classroom is his last alternative, after being in a behavior intervention class the year before. Although Ahmed seemed to be doing fine at the beginning of the semester, by the end of October his behavior has changed dramatically. He walks away from his desk while Ms. Cleary is teaching or when students are working independently. The ensuing conversation between Ms. Cleary and Ahmed can distract other classmates: "Ahmed, please go back to your seat and start reading with your reading partner." "Why? Why do I have to do that? I don't want to and I don't care about reading." At other times, Ahmed gets frustrated with other classmates and starts to shout: "Shut up! I don't want to hear what you say! I don't care!" If Ms. Cleary approaches Ahmed to take him out in the hallway, he shouts, "I hate her! I will do everything to hurt this girl!" Ms. Cleary sometimes takes him to Ms. Ward, a social worker for the school, whom Ahmed has been referred to since the beginning of November. Ms. Ward advised him to manage his anger by walking in the hallway to calm down. If this does not work, Ms. Cleary takes him again to see Ms. Ward for another solution. Academically, Ahmed is one of the three students in class who attends mainstream math class, which helps his self-confidence; however, he has a hard time reading and writing. Whenever he realizes that he cannot follow what other classmates are doing, his anger flares up. Ms. Cleary is concerned: How can Ahmed be included in the mainstream next year since he has spent more than two years in the immersion classroom? How can Ahmed's social behavior be improved so that there will be harmony within the classroom?

Note that students in Ms. Cleary's classroom will be either included in the mainstream classroom or repeat another year of English Immersion class when they start middle school (fifth grade). In preparation, the immersion classes are designed to develop literacy skills but do not have enough content in other academic areas. For example, the immersion classes use *Horizons*, a textbook designed to improve fluency skills by students answering the teacher-prompted questions. Because the *Horizons* teacher's guide tends to be very scripted, Ms. Cleary modifies questions and directions to be more interactive and engaging for students. Still, only a few passages contain a science or social studies aspect. For example, there is a story on how a boy and a girl rode on a time machine to go back to the time when Christopher Columbus reached America in 1492. However, the lesson does not explain the importance of the event in American history because its purpose is to improve reading fluency and not to focus on learning the historical content.

However, when students read about Egypt in *Horizons*, they showed quite an interest in learning about it so Ms. Cleary planned a unit about Egypt, mummies, and sphinxes. She incorporated world geography into the lesson on the seven continents. She did this during the "ESL period," which is 30 minutes of the day. She has the freedom to plan any lessons for ESL time and can incorporate a social studies component for the ESL period.

Low parental involvement is a persistent challenge. One time Ms. Cleary organized a Thanksgiving feast with two other English Immersion classes. She invited all the parents to join with their children; however, only one mother from Ms. Cleary's class came (a few parents participated from other classes). Because it was raining that day, the parents decided not to come to school, she thought. She was happy that some parents provided food for the feast by having their children bring it with them to school, although she was disappointed with the low attendance. In other years when she organized the same event, more parents had attended.

Ms. Cleary and the school try to organize events where the parents feel comfortable visiting the school. At the end of each month, classroom teachers nominate a student from each class who has demonstrated the three core values: *strive, succeed,* and *soar.* Parents of the recipients are encouraged to attend the ceremony as well. The nomination focuses not only on students' academic performance, but on the behavioral and social skills that each student demonstrates. The intention of the award is to motivate students to strive academically and socially. Receiving recognition in front of the school and their parents is the motivation to succeed. One day, Juliana was to receive this award. Juliana looked for her mother throughout the ceremony, only to find out that she was not there (although she had promised to come). Ms. Cleary understood Juliana's disappointment when it was her time to hand the award to Juliana. None of the parents from Ms. Cleary's class attended the school meeting for the award ceremony.

Ms. Cleary is also concerned that only three parents attended parent-teacher conferences this year. Taking parents' work schedules into consideration, the conferences were held in the evening. Ms. Cleary has had better years with higher parental involvement. This year was different.

Every day there is something that Ms. Cleary worries about. If Ahmed does well with his behavior, then the other students are pushing each other during transition. When the morning goes smoothly without any distraction from the students, some students are rambunctious during the recess. Although Ms. Cleary is quite confident about her teaching and she believes in students' abilities to succeed, there are days when she is disappointed and frustrated. She believes that understanding each student's family issues and language background and knowing about what other factors contribute to behavior are valuable information. She tries to communicate closely with each student to sense any difference in their lives. Since all the students in Ms. Cleary's class are starting middle school next year, she will have to decide who will be included in the mainstream classroom, as well as who should be recommended for another year of immersion class. "Are they ready for middle school?" she wonders. As she plans for the next day, she tells herself to be more patient with her students. She is also nervous about the preparation for the state exam starting in January.

## ■ Exhibit A: School Demographics

According to the school's Department of Education website, the total enrollment for a recent year was 415; 81 percent of students were Hispanic, followed by 7 percent white and 5 percent African-American. In terms of linguistic diversity, more than 80 percent of students spoke languages other than English as their first language, with about 30 percent of students identified as Limited English Proficient (LEP). In addition to language and cultural diversity, socioeconomic status is a factor at Stoney Hill: More than 90 percent of students come from low-income families. Based on these data and the fact that the majority of the population in the city is not born in the U.S., it is likely that the school represents the social diversity of the city.

Stoney Hill is rather a low-performing urban school compared to the national standard, and thus the curriculum for English immersion programs is heavily focused on literacy development. Although subjects other than math and language are provided, they are only offered 40 minutes a day as "specials" (science, music, art, or gym). These four subjects alternate each day. Therefore, students do not have access to social studies, history, or geography content unless the classroom teacher incorporates the content during writing workshops or ESL (refer to Exhibit C for the daily schedule).

## ■ Exhibit B: School Policies and Resources

The scores for third and fourth graders at Stoney Hill show that about 20 percent of students each year are failing in both English language arts and mathematics. This also holds true for the scores from the most recent academic year. Because of this phenomenon, class structure for students is heavily aimed at literacy development, with the daily schedule focusing on teaching math and language arts. To accommodate the linguistically, economically, and socially diverse community, the elementary school complex provides ample resources. For example, the library has a large number of books that are available to all students and their parents. A literacy program is offered for parents who wish to improve their English and get involved with their children's schoolwork, and students are eligible for extra assistance in math class after school.

To support the LEP population, the school district offers English immersion programs for each grade. At Stoney Hill, there are three different English immersion classes: a newcomers' program for Grades 3 and 4 combined called ELL 1; a class for Grade 3 called ELL 2; and a class for Grade 4 called ELL 3. This is because the school still faces the challenge of accommodating diverse needs, including high student mobility (moving from one district to another or one country to another). The student population in English immersion classes keeps growing; for example, ten new students joined one ELL class by the end of the school year.

## ■ Exhibit C: Daily Schedule

| | |
|---|---|
| 8:30–8:45 | Morning problem-solving (15 min.) |
| 8:45–9:45 | *Horizons*—reading comprehension, vocabulary, fluency (60 min.) |
| 9:45–10:40 | Writing workshop (55 min.) |
| 10:40–11:50 | Math (70 min.) |
| 11:50–12:20 | ESL (30 min.) |
| 12:20–13:00 | Lunch |
| 13:00–13:40 | Specials (rotate science, music, art, and gym) (40 min) |

## I. PRE-CASE DISCUSSION PROBLEMS SETS

Complete the chart after reading the case.

| Facts | |
|---|---|
| Opinions | |
| Assumptions | |
| Theories referred or connected to (if any) | |
| Ambiguous language | |
| Criteria you used in analyzing the case (e.g., emotional vs. rational) | |
| Emerging options | |

Write a pre-case discussion decision paper. Include these points:

   a. options for case resolution

   b. criteria (a rational decision should always be made with a set of criteria)

   c. analysis of options

   d. recommendation (of the best choice among the options)

   e. action plan

## II. CASE DISCUSSION QUESTIONS

### Big-Picture Analysis

Describe the context of the case.

- student demographics
- the school district
- Stoney Hill scheduling changes
- state and federal policy mandates
- administrative constraints
- curriculum

### Stakeholders

In small groups, assume the role of one of the case stakeholders. Write a statement/dialogue expressing this person's or group's hypothetical feelings and perspectives. Be prepared to act out your roles to the large group.

- Ms. Cleary
- school administrators
- Ahmed
- Juliana
- parents
- the rest of the students in the class

### Surface Issues

What are the surface issues in this case? What is happening here from an untrained perspective? What underlying assumptions or beliefs feed into this perspective?

### Deep Issues

Discuss the real issues in the case. Try to categorize them in terms of language teaching curriculum and instruction.

### Evidence-Based Solutions

In groups, develop evidence-based solutions for each deep issue listed. Whenever possible, refer to a theory or principle of language learning and teaching to support your proposed solutions.

### Teacher Thinking

In what ways does this case influence and/or reinforce your beliefs and dispositions as a teacher? Consult the Further Resources section to help with theoretically informed solutions.

## III. POST-CASE PROBLEM SETS

### Post-Case Analysis

A. Categorize what you learned as:
- teacher knowledge and praxis (e.g., content knowledge, curricular knowledge, pedagogical content knowledge and application)
- teacher thinking (e.g., beliefs, problem-solving strategies, prioritizing objectives, values, professional ethics, attitudes)

B. List:
- learning objectives that you discovered in the case
- potential learning outcomes
- implications for your pedagogical practices

C. The post-case problem sets introduce reactions from various perspectives. These quotes are from others who have read the cases for educational and pedagogical purposes. Read all of the quotes and then choose two about which to write a short response (put the quotes at the top of each response).  Use these questions as a guide:

- What is the message the speaker is trying to convey? If possible, also explain why you chose the quote.
- What examples can you think of that connect to the themes presented?
- Can you relate the quote to a class discussion or to something you have read or experienced?

Quotes

1. "It would be valuable for the teacher to gather information about Ahmed's background to determine what might be causing his anger and his outbursts. If Ahmed is coming from a violent or messy situation in his home country or faces extracurricular responsibilities or stresses at home, knowing about it might be a good way to take steps to deal with his behavior issues in class. Overall, the teacher should know her students better."

2. "My recommendation for this teacher is to be tougher with her class as a whole: If students are spiteful or fail to follow directions, I would ask them do the task over and over and over again until they've got it right. Even if it takes two weeks or longer or if it takes away from instruction, I would still do that. After all, the disruptive behaviors take away from instruction as it is, and things can't be allowed to go on like that. I will set my expectations as the teacher high and explicitly tell them what the rules and the consequences are. We will practice proper protocol and appropriate listening and speaking until we get it right. If they are stubborn, this might backfire, but maybe these are kids who are pushing their boundaries to see how far they can go. And just maybe, the boundaries need to be made as firm as can be so that these students realize that rules are rules!"

3. "Perhaps, Ms. Cleary should incorporate more on-task or hands-on activities, which involve critical and creative thinking. Also, the teacher can incorporate more peer-to-peer interaction so that the students have more of a purpose for discussion rather

than disrupting the class. Students at that age probably have a lot of unanswered questions so the teacher should encourage students to ask questions. This way, a discussion can be initiated, and students can take turns expressing their opinion or thoughts. It might be difficult for her to incorporate such activities because she is dealing with a variety of students from different backgrounds, which means they have different learning styles. Despite the fact that the students are active and talkative, they may not have anything to say if the class was discussing verbs or multiplying fractions. At that age, the students are most likely extrinsically motivated so even though it might be helpful for these students to realize the purposes of some of the activities, they will most likely need an incentive to even begin a certain activity.

Additionally, even with the mini-lessons on social studies topics that she is able to incorporate into her English language arts or math lessons, there is too much focus on the subjects covered on the MCAS [statewide assessment] and a stark disregard for social studies. A balance needs to be found between placing an emphasis on the statewide assessment subjects and still being able to incorporate social studies in the daily curriculum. Without a solid and consistent addition of social studies, there is no way for the students to be prepared to enter a mainstream environment in the middle school years. To be successful in middle school (and to be good citizens), the students also need some social studies—and more science. When they get to middle school they're going to be at a disadvantage when they're mainstreamed, as not only will their English probably be less proficient that their peers', but also their social studies and science knowledge will be lacking. Ms. Cleary does not have much 'wriggle room' in the curriculum/ schedule to remedy this."

4. "Many of the parents have to work during the day—some at jobs with extremely long hours. It is difficult for them to come to school during the day to participate in activities even if they might like to. The teacher should try providing alternative times for the parents to come and get involved at the school; perhaps hosting some activities after or before school when more parents might be able to come."

D. Write a reflection describing a take-away from the case in terms of praxis. Make sure to develop an action plan to resolve the case. Consider these questions as guidelines:

- In what ways did the case discussion influence your thinking about the case?
- Did you change your original decision or did the discussion reaffirm your position?
- What points had you not considered prior to the case discussion?
- How might the information you gained from this case be applicable to your current instructional setting and/or future instructional settings?
- What did you learn?
- What are you inspired to learn more about?
- How did the themes discussed in class apply to your experience?

E. Discuss what theoretical basis there is for:

- the stakeholders' behavior in the case.
- the solutions you proposed.

## Further Reading and Resources

Coleman, R., & Goldenberg, C. (2012). The common core challenge for ELLs. *Principal Leadership, 4*(5), 46–51.

De Gaetano, Y. (2007). The role of culture in engaging Latino parents' involvement in school. *Urban Education, 42*, 145–162.

DeCapua, A., Smathers, W., & L. F. Tang. (2009). *Meeting the needs of students with limited or interrupted schooling: A guide for educators.* Ann Arbor: University of Michigan Press.

Echevaria, J., Vogt, M., & Short, D. (2013). *Making content comprehensible for English learners: The SIOP model.* Upper Saddle River, NJ: Pearson.

Gottlieb, M. (2006). *Assessing English language learners: Bridges from language proficiency to academic achievement.* Thousand Oaks, CA: Corwin Press.

Haynes, J., & Zacarian, D. (2010). *Teaching English language learners across the content areas.* Alexandria, VA: ASCD.

Herczog, M. (2012). What's our objective for English learners? Preparation for college, career, and citizenship via language objectives and research-based instruction. *Social Studies Review, 51*(1), 89–93.

Hoare, P., Kong, S., & Bell, J. (2008). Using language objectives to integrate language and content instruction: A case history of planning and implementation challenges. *Language and Education*, *22*(3), 187–206.

Ramirez, A.Y. (2008). Immigrant families and schools: The need for a better relationship. In T.Turner-Vorbeck & M. M. March (Eds.), *Other kinds of families: Diversity in schools and culture* (pp. 28–45). New York: Teachers College Press.

Snow, M.A., & Brinton, D. (2017). *The content-based classroom* (Second Ed.). Ann Arbor: University of Michigan Press.

Turner-Vorbeck, T., & March, M.M. (Eds.). *Other kinds of families: Diversity in schools and culture* (pp. 28–45). New York: Teachers College Press.

# ▪▪▪▪▪▪▪▪▪▪▪▪▪▪▪▪ CASE 2.2 ▪▪▪▪▪▪▪▪▪▪▪▪▪▪▪▪

# Dean School

Ms. Thomas is sitting in her empty classroom staring at her lesson plans. She has open before her the teacher's manuals for two different school-required literacy programs (*Into English* and *Reach and Learn*) and, as usual, is having trouble with the day's lesson plans. She recognizes the value in focusing on promoting literacy in her classroom but feels that the students are receiving disjointed instruction, while lacking all of the social studies and science curriculum of the mainstream second grade classroom. Glancing at lessons in the teacher's manuals, she tries to think of a way to include the literacy content for this lesson into a unit that fits within the larger framework for second grade science or social studies. She sighs in surrender. She knows that she has to follow the two literacy curricula exactly, that she doesn't have enough time in the day to include elements from the mainstream curriculum, and that her schedule will not allow her any flexibility in terms of what will be taught. She must stick to literacy instruction, with a brief 40 minutes devoted to math after lunch. She closes the book and moves to stand by the door, waiting for the students to arrive.

All of the sheltered immersion classrooms at Dean School work with the state-mandated curriculum. Ms. Thomas teaches the second grade sheltered immersion program. Most of her students completed the first year of sheltered English immersion at the school, but a few are new to the program this year, and there is even one student who arrived a few weeks ago. Her classroom has 15 students: Some come from various Latin American countries and all speak Spanish. The others are from Sudan, Nepal, Cambodia, Côte d'Ivoire, and Somalia. The students in her class are all at vastly different levels of spoken and written English proficiency. The range of literacy levels is wide, with one student still working on his letter sounds and others who are reading at a second grade level. Here is a look at four struggling ELLs in her class:

1. Ana is from Colombia. She is the youngest in the class. She is a sweet, bright little girl who loves to hug, hold hands with, or lean against her friends and teachers. She is always asking for help with work because she doesn't "know what to do," yet she does just fine if coaxed to think about the assignment and try to figure it out on her own. She loves to draw and color, one activity she never hesitates with. According to WIDA levels, Ana is labeled as an ELD Level 2.

2. Heeta has great trouble sitting still. She is constantly squirming and appears to drift a lot during instruction. A recently settled refugee from Somalia whose family is still adjusting to their new country, she enrolled in school last year, which was her first exposure to print or school practices. When she first arrived in the classroom, she needed help learning how to hold a pencil and understanding print concepts, like reading left to right. She keeps to herself and doesn't seem to connect with the other children in class. The girls are friendly and willing to include her in their group at recess time, but Heeta would rather help the teacher. Because she has to be called to attention, Heeta doesn't do as well academically as she could, even though her oral English is quite good. While her overall WIDA ELD level is 3, her Speaking and Listening score is 4, and her Reading and Writing score is 1.

3. Lukerson is an extremely quiet boy from Haiti who is on an Individual Education Plan. He appears to have issues with fine motor skills and speech problems, plus language limitations. Unlike Heeta who can't sit still for long, Lukerson sits stiffly during instruction, seemingly staring at something only he sees, and sometimes drums the tips of his fingers together or rubs them hard against one of his palms or thighs. He hardly ever volunteers answers unless coaxed by the teacher, and when he speaks, it's always one-word and staccato. According to Ms. Thomas, he's made amazing progress in the 10 weeks since he was placed in her classroom. His reading fluency is improving, and his writing is still emerging. He needs to approach every task in steps and lags behind his peers who are at grade level. He almost only plays with one boy, Tiago, during recess, and his Individual Education Plan notes that his social skills are sorely lacking.

4. Tiago is a bubbly boy whose reading seemed to improve after getting prescription glasses. He arrived from Brazil eight months ago where he attended school inconsistently. Like Heeta, he can't sit still, lacks focus, and has to be called to attention by the teacher. Tiago is social and very friendly and will play with the girls or the other boys, although he's been recently "adopted" by Lukerson and has been playing more with him than with the other three boys in the class. He seems to struggle with understanding classroom norms and expectations. For example, he often disrupts the teacher during read-alouds and makes off-the-topic comments.

Out of the four, Heeta is the only one who doesn't have very low oral language skills in English. However, all four are lagging behind academically, and the problem is compounded by the fact that they can't seem to focus for long and often move their bodies to the point of distraction. They are all emergent writers: During writing workshop, they draw more pictures than they write words to tell their stories. The two girls have better letter formation than the two boys.

Ms. Thomas must strictly follow the *Into English* and the *Reach and Learn* reading curricula.

The school day is broken into 40-minute blocks for each subject. Ms. Thomas instructs reading from 8:30–10:00. Then the students go to "Specials" from 10:00–10:40, return to the classroom at 10:40, and do reading workshop until 11:20. Following workshop, there is recess from 12:00 until 12:15. They eat lunch from 12:15 until 12:40. After lunch is math from 12:40 until 1:40 and, finally, writing from 1:40 until dismissal at 2:30. This schedule is heavy on literacy instruction, with just the short break for mathematics in the afternoon. The class schedule must be strictly adhered to. Ms. Thomas is unable to change the times of any of the subjects. She finds the morning schedule particularly long. She sees the importance of providing students with large blocks of time to practice reading and writing skills, but she would not have designed the schedule in such a way if given a choice. The current schedule requires focus for several hours without any outlets for physical movement. It is common for students to lose focus by the end of the morning. In fact, one boy will sometimes stop looking at her completely and lose himself in daydreaming or drawing pictures no matter what she tries to do to pull his attention back.

The 15-minute recess is barely enough to allow the children to get outside and begin running around before they are asked to line up again. It is difficult to keep the children focused on their school work in the workshop period just before recess and lunch. The more excitable children are constantly asking "When is lunch?" while nearly bouncing off the walls and failing completely to focus on their work in the hour before lunch. Also, the lunch break is relatively long so most students finish well before the half-hour allotment, but they are forced to sit in the cafeteria after finishing lunch. They are not allowed to get up, although there is sometimes 15 minutes after eating. Ms. Thomas often comes into the cafeteria to find some of her students getting into trouble. Once, she caught two students having a food fight.

During the reading period, the students are divided into two groups. The lower literacy group stays with Ms. Thomas and works with the *Reach and Learn* reading curriculum, while the higher literacy group leaves the classroom to work with a reading teacher. They use the same program but at a higher level. This is a convenient arrangement because it very neatly differentiates the classroom. It is a particularly good time for the class to break into small groups because reading instruction is one of the cornerstones of the sheltered immersion curriculum at Dean School. Even so, some of the kids, like Jamal, fall behind. Jamal is still working on his letter sounds, and he does not always understand the work of the lower literacy group.

The literacy materials and curriculum assigned drive the progresses, and each set of materials works under a different unit theme. Because the reading curriculum is derived from several different instructional guides with themes like "lucky numbers" or "the weather," Ms. Thomas is forced to use a different theme for each period of her day. Each subject taught has a different mini-theme for the unit. The mini-themes prescribed by the instructional materials are not consistent with the state's frameworks for grade-level content. Ms. Thomas' learning objectives must focus exclusively on addressing the English Language Proficiency Benchmarks and Outcomes for ELLs. There is no extra time in the schedule for the instruction in the content areas. As a result, students will enter the upper elementary grades missing parts of the first and second grade curricula. Their grade-level peers are participating in long lessons on science and social studies. Ms. Thomas tries to include some pieces of a social studies curriculum in her classroom by doing the occasional read-aloud book on a different second-grade social studies topic. She used to teach in a different school that followed a theme-based curriculum. She misses seeing her students being exposed to as many as four different unit themes per day. Ms. Thomas is worried that the students will be unprepared for the mainstream classroom that many of them will enter next year. She knows that the few read-alouds she has done in her classroom on content area topics are not nearly sufficient to get them up to speed in either of these subjects.

At Dean School, Ms. Thomas must also teach at a specific pace; she is not able to stop or slow down if students are falling behind because she has to meet standards set by the school. The students have to receive a certain amount of material and instruction before finishing the year in her classroom, whether they have fully mastered all the content or not. Usually, the material requires teaching a new concept each day. Many times she has looked up after giving a math lesson to see the blank faces of the students. Some of the more vocal students will even raise their hands and say things like, "Miss, I don't understand!" Many students are not ready to progress to a new topic each day, and this is particularly evident in the math period. Most of the students in Ms. Thomas' class do not fully master the topic that is introduced on any given day, so reviewing the preceding day's material is critical, but the math curriculum does not provide review materials per topic until the end of a unit. Ms. Thomas often falls behind when she provides students with review of the already learned material and then does not have time to teach the new concept for the day.

The Dean School is attempting to deal with the challenges of an ESL sheltered immersion classroom with an assigned curriculum and schedule. The school strives to perform well on statewide mandates and, since ELLs tend to perform poorly on these exams, the administration has decided to schedule a rigorous literacy curriculum aligned with Common Core standards. Most of the lessons include practice with literacy strategies, such as finding the main idea, scanning for details, and identifying author purpose. Ms. Thomas struggles with ways to allow her students to learn the necessary literacy skills while still providing them with rich, authentic content on grade-level material.

Both of the English programs that she uses are effective and comprehensive. She likes using them, but she wishes she could supplement them with more materials or design her own plan of study. Every day when Ms. Thomas sits down to write her lessons she is confronted with the same problems: How can she give students adequate literacy practice while not neglecting the instruction of important grade-level curriculum? She is at a loss for the best way to deal with all of the different constraints placed on her by the school, the curriculum, and the students.

## ■ Exhibit A: Dean School—Mission Statement

All students in the school will advance their academic and social skills to achieve grade-level or higher benchmarks. Students will be prepared to reach the proficient level on state-mandated tests (MCAS) and locally developed assessments. The school aims to develop and expand all students' literacy and mathematics skills, promote student emotional and social development, and encourage parental involvement to build a home-and-school partnership for academic success.

## ■ Exhibit B: School Curriculum

The Dean School is an elementary school located in an urban area comprised mainly of immigrants. This area is predominantly Hispanic although there are families from all over the world, including many from different parts of Africa and Asia. Many of the students are the sons and daughters of immigrants or immigrants themselves. These children all come from very different backgrounds and have very different learning needs. This population includes many refugees who were forced to flee their countries. Newly arrived students of all different ages and educational backgrounds constantly enter the school throughout the year.

To address the needs of these children the school has a number of ESL classrooms. Services are provided for these students in sheltered English immersion classrooms, of which there are three levels. The newest immigrants, or those with the most limited English language skills, are placed in Level 1 immersion classrooms, and then they move into Levels 2 and 3 for their second year of schooling in the United States.

After one year in the sheltered immersion program, students are evaluated. Some have sufficient English proficiency and move into the mainstream classroom for the next academic year, but this is not very common, as the students usually need services for multiple years. The state requires that the ELLs become proficient in English "very soon" after their arrival in the country, so there is enormous pressure on the sheltered immersion teachers to push students through the program. To move students into mainstream classrooms quickly, the instructors must teach mandated curriculum and literacy skills rapidly, often at the expense of thoroughness.

There is no specific policy as to where or in what level a newly arrived student will be placed. A student's school records are examined, and English proficiency is briefly assessed by the administration. The student is then placed in an immersion classroom. Some students are placed in a higher- or lower-level English class than befits their skills because of age constraints.

In addition to placing the newly arrived students, the administration assigns the daily schedules and specific literacy curriculum to each sheltered immersion classroom. The teachers in these classrooms are required to teach reading and English using only the prescribed curriculum. The required programs for the literacy curriculum at the school are: *Reach and Learn* and *Into English* or *Amazing English*.

The *Reach and Learn* reading program is designed for first graders. It combines systematic phonics instruction with authentic literature and is theme-based. Different authentic texts are presented with phonics. The 90-minute reading block assigned by the administration consists of 40 minutes of reading comprehension strategy instruction using read-alouds followed by time for students to independently practice the daily phonics concept.

Various supplemental materials are provided with the *Reach and Learn* program. At the beginning of the year, the program focuses on using *Big Books*® to engage non-readers, develop print awareness, and to teach students to participate in good reading behaviors. During that time, the teacher instructs students how to respond to both literature and expository texts before they are actually able to read themselves. The teacher also demonstrates what good readers do by modeling strategies for the class. These strategies include: asking concept questions about the text, making predictions, making clarifications while reading, and doing think-alouds about a text.

In addition to *Big Books*®, books that practice decoding are provided so students can individually practice the phonics concepts. Sound/spelling cards are available for student reference to use while practicing independent decoding. Stories in the books focusing on decoding build on prior phonics knowledge and provide a focus on one new sound concept. The books for students to read independently are generally extremely simple texts with a sometimes exaggerated incorporation of a particular phonetic sound. The focus of these books is the sounds, not the story-lines, and so the characters and the plot receive little attention and are often poorly developed. The students read a different book each day.

The final component of the *Reach and Learn* program, which comes near the end of the year, is student anthologies. These anthologies provide students with one story each week that goes along with the unit theme and ask students to prac-tice the various reading comprehension strategies. Students begin using them after a sufficient amount of time has been spent on modeling good reading practices. The teachers must follow the program instructions exactly, even reading the pro-vided prompts from the teacher's manual.

The second literacy program the school uses is called *Into English*. It also uses thematic units and provides literature for any age level. This program was designed specifically for ELLs and bilingual students. It attempts to integrate the different language skills while presenting grade-level content and using hands-on learning and authentic assessments. The students are not provided with books in this pro-gram. The teacher is given an instructor's manual, which provides explicit instruc-tions for each lesson. The goal of this program is to help students develop grade-level academic language and give students access to the core curriculum. The program uses a lot of visuals and literature, all designed specifically for ELLs, including posters and *Big Books®*. It also tries to promote phonemic awareness and provide some phonics instruction through sing-alongs, rhymes, and CDs. There are also *Patterned Books®* to develop print concepts and reading strategies. *Language Logs®* are also used, which allow students to independently practice the lesson concepts.

## ■ Exhibit C: Themes for Required School Literacy Curriculum

Mini-Themes for *Reach and Learn:*

> Unit 1: Let's Read
> Unit 2: Animals
> Unit 3: Things That Go
> Unit 4: Our Neighborhood at Work
> Unit 5: Weather
> Unit 6: Journeys
> Unit 7: Keep Trying
> Unit 8: Games
> Unit 9: Being Afraid
> Unit 10: Homes

Mini-Themes for *Into English* series:

> *Best foot forward*—clothes, careers, activities, and mail
> *A walk in the woods*—animals, ocean animals, habitats
> *One to grow on*—plants, fruits, vegetables, body parts, insects, senses, buying and selling
> *Under construction*—introduction to communities, building, houses
> *Just around the corner*—communities, city features, neighborhood places, goods and services, signs, errands, transportation, family members, family activities
> *Farm fresh*—farm animals, animal sounds, animal characteristics, vegetables, fruits, living and non-living things, parts of the body

## ▮ Exhibit D: DOE Curriculum Frameworks for Social Studies Grade 2 (www.doe.mass.edu)

Students should be able to apply concepts and skills learned in previous grades:

### History and Geography

1. Use a calendar to identify days, weeks, months, years, and seasons.

2. Use correctly words and phrases related to time *(now, in the past, in the future)*, changing historical periods *(other times, other places)*, and causation *(because, reasons)*.

3. Explain the information that historical timelines convey and then put in chronological order events in the student's life (e.g., the year he or she was born, started school, or moved to a new neighborhood) or in the history of countries studied.

4. Describe how maps and globes depict geographical information in different ways.

5. Read globes and maps and follow narrative accounts using them.

### Civics and Government

6. Define and give examples of some of the rights and responsibilities that students as citizens have in the school (e.g., students have the right to vote in a class election and have the responsibility to follow school rules).

7. Give examples of fictional characters or real people in the school or community who were good leaders and good citizens, and explain the qualities that made them admirable (e.g., honesty, dependability, modesty, trustworthiness, courage).

**Economics**

8. Give examples of people in the school and community who are both producers and consumers.

9. Explain what buyers and sellers are and give examples of goods and services that are bought and sold in their community.

### Grade 2 Learning Standards

Building on knowledge from previous years, students should be able to:

2.1 On a map of the world, locate all of the continents: North America, South America, Europe, Asia, Africa, Australia, and Antarctica.

2.2 Locate the current boundaries of the United States, Canada, and Mexico.

2.3 Locate the oceans of the world: the Arctic, Atlantic, Indian, Pacific, and Southern Oceans.

2.4 Locate five major rivers in the world: the Mississippi, Amazon, Volga, Yangtze, and Nile.

2.5 Locate major mountains or mountain ranges in the world such as the Andes, Alps, Himalayas, Mt. Everest, Mt. Denali, and the Rocky Mountains.

2.6 Explain the difference between a continent and a country and give examples of each.

2.7 On a map of the world, locate the continent, regions, or countries from which students, their parents, guardians, grandparents, or other relatives or ancestors came. With the help of family members and the school librarian, describe traditional food, customs, sports and games, and music of the place they came from.

2.8 With the help of the school librarian, give examples of traditions or customs from other countries that can be found in America today.

2.9 With the help of the school librarian, identify and describe well-known sites, events, or landmarks in at least three different countries from which students' families come and explain why they are important.

2.10 After reading or listening to a variety of true stories about individuals recognized for their achievements, describe and compare different ways people have achieved great distinction (e.g., scientific, professional, political, religious, commercial, military, athletic, or artistic).

## I. PRE-CASE DISCUSSION PROBLEMS SETS

Complete the chart after reading the case.

| | |
|---|---|
| Facts | |
| Opinions | |
| Assumptions | |
| Theories referred or connected to (if any) | |
| Ambiguous language | |
| Criteria you used in analyzing the case (e.g., emotional vs. rational) | |
| Emerging options | |

Write a pre-case discussion decision paper. Include these points:

a. options for case resolution

b. criteria (a rational decision should always be made with a set of criteria)

c. analysis of options

d. recommendation (of the best choice among the options)

e. action plan

## II. CASE DISCUSSION QUESTIONS

### Big-Picture Analysis

Describe the context of the case.

- policy context: No Child Left Behind and English Only Initiative
- curricular context: sheltered English immersion model
- teaching and learning climate at the Dean School
- student demographics

### Stakeholders

In small groups, assume the role of one of the case stakeholders. Write a statement/ dialogue expressing this person's or group's hypothetical feelings and perspectives. Be prepared to act out your roles to the large group.

- Ms. Thomas
- Dean School administrators
- Ana
- Heeta
- Lukerson
- Tiago

### Surface Issues

What are the surface issues in this case? What is happening here from an untrained perspective? What underlying assumptions or beliefs feed into this perspective?

### Deep Issues

Discuss the real issues in the case. Try to categorize them in terms of language teaching curriculum and instruction.

### *Evidence-Based Solutions*

In groups, develop evidence-based solutions for each deep issue listed. Whenever possible, refer to a theory or principle of language learning and teaching to support your proposed solutions.

### *Teacher Thinking*

In what ways does this case influence and/or reinforce your beliefs and dispositions as a teacher? Consult the Further Resources section to help with theoretically informed solutions.

## III. POST-CASE PROBLEM SETS

### *Post-Case Analysis*

A. Categorize what you learned as:

- teacher knowledge and praxis (e.g., content knowledge, curricular knowledge, pedagogical content knowledge and application)
- teacher thinking (e.g., beliefs, problem-solving strategies, prioritizing objectives, values, professional ethics, attitudes)

B. List:

- learning objectives that you discovered in the case
- potential learning outcomes
- implications for your pedagogical practices

C. The post-case problem sets introduce reactions from various perspectives. These quotes are from others who have read the cases for educational and pedagogical purposes. Read all of the quotes and then choose two about which to write a short response (put the quotes at the top of each response). Use these questions as a guide:

- What is the message the speaker is trying to convey? If possible, also explain why you chose the quote.
- What examples can you think of that connect to the themes presented?
- Can you relate the quote to a class discussion or to something you have read or experienced?

Quotes

1. "As it was mentioned in the case study, students were misbehaving during lunch, which is the only time of the day when they can release their energy. While many other suburban schools implement snack time during the middle of morning schedules, Dean School second graders do not have any break until lunch period. A certain amount of time for ventilation is effective on students' learning as much as it is for adults. Cramming students with literacy instruction all in the morning simply uses up their energy and brainpower, which results in not having enough motivation and energy to work on their writing skills in the afternoon. Changing schedules is important but not within the teacher's jurisdiction."

2. "If Ms. Thomas wants to keep her job, she just has to stick to the curriculum. If not, she should look to teach elsewhere."

3. "There are opportunities to develop a theme-based lesson even with the curriculum she currently has to teach. With a little creativity, she could bring in authentic, supplementary materials that would connect to grade-level content."

4. "Sometimes teachers think that they have to follow a curriculum exactly the way it is presented, but this is not always the case. Ms. Thomas should just talk to her principal and have a candid discussion about the challenges she is facing due to varying learner profiles."

5. "This case highlights the negative impacts of standards-based testing on ELL teaching and learning. Our education policy has to change in order to better support, rather than hurt, our immigrant students and their teachers."

D. Write a reflection describing a take-away from the case in terms of praxis. Make sure to develop an action plan to resolve the case. Consider these questions as guidelines:

- In what ways did the case discussion influence your thinking about the case?
- Did you change your original decision or did the discussion reaffirm your position?
- What points had you not considered prior to the case discussion?

- How might the information you gained from this case be applicable to your current instructional setting and/or future instructional settings?
- What did you learn?
- What are you inspired to learn more about?
- How did the themes discussed in class apply to your experience?

E. Discuss what theoretical basis there is for:

- the stakeholders' behavior in the case.
- the solutions you proposed.

## Further Reading and Resources

Coleman, R., & Goldenberg, C. (2010). What does research say about effective practices for ELLs. *Kappa Delta Pi Record, 46*(2), 60–65.

Echevarria, J., & Graves, A. (2011). Sheltered instruction in the content areas. In *Sheltered content instruction: Teaching English learners with diverse abilities* (4th ed., pp. 44–54). Boston: Pearson.

Tabors, P. (2008). *One child, two languages: A guide for early childhood educators of children learning English as a second language* (2nd ed.). Baltimore, MD: Paul Brookes Publishers.

WIDA English Language Proficiency Standards. (2007 and 2012). Available at www.wida.us

Wright, W. E. (2010). *Foundations for teaching English language learners: Research, theory, policy, and practice.* Philadelphia: Caslon Publishing.

# ■■■■■■■■■■■■■■■ CASE 2.3 ■■■■■■■■■■■■■■■
# Hanlen School

Hanlen is a school in the northwest suburb of a major city that is the smallest of three elementary schools in the town with about 200 K–5 students. Over the years, the number of children who do not speak English at home has been increasing all over the town. This particular school has two apartment complexes popular with new arrivals from other countries in its district, so 25 percent of the students have a home language other than English. Most of these students are from the Indian subcontinent and speak a variety of languages. Despite the large number of these students, only about 25 percent of them are in the ELL program, because many of the parents are well-educated so their children have learned English.

Besides the ELL program, there are other support services for students: reading teachers, literacy tutors, math coaches, math tutors, speech and language teachers, and the learning center staffed by a teacher qualified in special education. To receive services in the learning center a student must have an individualized learning plan. The ELL, reading, literacy, and speech and language teachers either work in the classroom with the student(s) or pull them out to work individually or in small groups.

School policies (see Exhibit B) have been in place and generally adhered to until the arrival of a new superintendent this year. In the new superintendent's former district, in Virginia, the old model of help for lagging students (similar to the synchronous online communication design) was not working, so they started a specialized approach to literacy development for struggling readers (or Response to Intervention program) (see Exhibit C). As a result, this same program is now mandated for use in this district. At a presentation on Response to Intervention (RTI), teachers were told: "Don't think outside the box. Throw the old box away!"

At this school the online communication forum is in limbo, and procedures for RTI are not fully understood by all in the district. The classroom to which Medha was assigned is staffed by two very experienced teachers. There are about 16 students in the room, four of whom have been designated LEP. A few others' home language is not English. Three of the four LEP students are from the Indian subcontinent and speak Bengali, Sindhi, and Telegu. The fourth is from Somalia and is repeating kindergarten. Although not fully qualified to teach LEP students (as recognized by the DOE), the teachers have a great deal of teaching experience, including teaching ELL students. They are soft-spoken, calm, and firm about expectations.

Medha entered kindergarten in September. Her fifth birthday was at the end of June, so she is at the young end of the group. She was born in the United States, but her mother noted on the home language survey that Sindhi is her first language and what is used at home. Medha was duly screened for English proficiency. The screener noted that it was very hard to keep her focused on the task and that she was easily distracted. Medha was unable to answer the items that required concentration, such as repeating a sentence or answering questions about a short story. Consequently she was designated LEP, and a letter was sent to her parents stating that she would be receiving extra help.

Before school started, Medha's mother phoned to tell the ELL teacher that Medha did not speak English at home. She stated that Medha often might not understand what was said, so things needed to be repeated several times.

When ELL instruction began, Medha wore glasses. They are bifocals. Medha seemed to have difficulty seeing pictures in books or flashcards. The classroom teacher spoke to the mother, who said that the girl only needed glasses because of a lazy eye. This difficulty persisted, however. It was also apparent that Medha often jerked or twitched. At the kindergarten screening in mid-September, these things were noted, as were other anomalies. All observations were reported to the ELL teacher by the classroom teacher, but the ELL teacher did not see the actual screening form.

For the first few months, Medha was seen by the ELL teacher with another student from the class, the boy from Somalia. The two children got on well together and were respectful of each other. At first it seemed that Medha had a lot of vocabulary gaps, but when she was able to focus properly on the flashcard or picture, it became apparent that it was more a question of not seeing than not knowing the word.

However, two other behaviors were much more problematic. The first was that Medha found it difficult to bring her attention to the work to be done. She had to be constantly refocused and just saying her name is insufficient. Sometimes her hand has to be touched to bring her back to the job at hand. It can take her at least 10 minutes to write her name because she gazes off into space or discusses what she should do next. The teacher reports that she never finishes any task. If she is coloring, unless she is told a specific color to use, she will take minutes to decide on one. This also applies when choosing a book in the library. Because the ELL teacher was able to do much less in the allotted time with Medha than with other children, the schedule was rearranged so that Medha would be instructed on her own.

The second problem is that, although Medha can speak fairly fluently, what she says does not make sense. Sometimes the sentences themselves are totally incomprehensible. Sometimes the sentences are grammatically correct, but the vocabulary is inappropriate. Sometimes the sentences are completely fine, but they do not relate to anything being done at that time. At times a relationship can be seen between what Medha is saying and something done previously, but at other times what she says seems completely random. For example, she will tell stories from an imaginary world and digress. In her state oral proficiency assessment in October, the kindergarten teacher did not want to give her a score for comprehension because Medha's responses often did not relate to directions given or questions asked, and the teacher was unsure if this was a comprehension or a distractibility issue.

As a result, Medha's case was brought to the online communication forum. Besides the ELL and classroom teachers, others present at the meeting had witnessed these problems. It was decided that the speech and language teacher should evaluate her and that another meeting should be arranged in the future to discuss further procedures.

The ELL teacher is unsure how to move forward in terms of focus and English learning.

### ▊ Exhibit A: School Profile

The ELL population has increased, so the ELL program has grown bit by bit. For the four elementary schools, two elementary ELL teachers serve two schools. One ELL teacher is full time and the other has a 70 percent position. Students are placed in a mainstream classroom and pulled out for individual or small group ELL instruction in 30-minute blocks two or three times a week. Some of the teachers have SEI training, but not everyone, and so, by the Department of Education standards, are not fully qualified to teach ELL students. The classroom size in this school is quite small, 15 to 17 students, and in the kindergarten classroom there is also a qualified aide who works with the teacher. Kindergarten teachers also welcome parent volunteers to help the students with their classroom projects, so the adult/child ratio is good.

### ▊ Exhibit B: School Policies

When a student is registered at school, the parents must complete a home language survey. If the answer to any of the questions is a language other than English, then that child is screened for English proficiency. For kindergarteners, this is an oral test that checks vocabulary, verb tenses, prepositions, plurals, ability to ask questions, recall of a 5-sentence story, etc. If the student's score does not put them in the fluent category, then they are designated LEP and will join the ELL program. A letter is sent home to the parents informing them that their child will be receiving extra help with his/her English and what they should do if they do not want this service.

As LEP students are seen individually or in small groups, the program is customized for each student/group. For students in Grade 1 and higher, *Let's Go* is the basis for grammar, the *Oxford Picture Dictionary for Kids* is the basis for vocabulary, and *Classic Tales* is the basis for reading and culture, although many other texts are also used. In kindergarten the emphasis is more on teaching vocabulary and culture, as all the children are learning literacy together in the classroom. Flashcards, realia, poetry, pictures, and games are used. Many of the ELLs do not know basic vocabulary (clothes, parts of body, household words, etc.) as those are the words usually learned at home, so that is an important piece. The ELL teacher also coordinates with the kindergarten teacher to reinforce vocabulary and concepts being taught in the classroom.

At the elementary level, report cards are sent home three times a year, and the ELL teacher writes a report separate from the classroom progress report. At that time, the ELL teacher looks at the student's progress through the ELL benchmarks with the classroom teacher. The benchmarks are used as a checklist to ensure that they are not only being adhered to as required by the DOE but also that progress is being made.

The ELL and classroom teachers discuss the academic content that the LEP student needs and, frequently, also the behavior and progress of the students. If a student is having difficulty, there are guidelines for how to proceed. The first step is to bring the student's case to an assessment committee comprised of the guidance counselor, two or three classroom teachers, the special education teacher, and sometimes the principal or someone from administration. The teacher of the student presents the problem, and, if the student is LEP, the ELL teacher also adds what she sees. Then the group discusses the best way to proceed. If the student is LEP, lack of English is often seen as the cause of all the problems.

### ■ Exhibit C: Response and Intervention

Readers should consult www.rtinetwork.org to familiarize themselves with the process.

## I. PRE-CASE DISCUSSION PROBLEMS SETS

Complete the chart after reading the case.

| | |
|---|---|
| Facts | |
| Opinions | |
| Assumptions | |
| Theories referred or connected to (if any) | |
| Ambiguous language | |
| Criteria you used in analyzing the case (e.g., emotional vs. rational) | |
| Emerging options | |

Write a pre-case discussion decision paper. Include these points:

a. options for case resolution

b. criteria (a rational decision should always be made with a set of criteria)

c. analysis of options

d. recommendation (of the best choice among the options)

e. action plan

## II. CASE DISCUSSION QUESTIONS

### Big-Picture Analysis

Describe the context of the case. Discuss the school structure and curricular model.

### Stakeholders

What do we know about the ESL teacher? What information does the case present about Medha and her mother? What new change has the superintendent brought this year, and what are the benefits and challenges of this change for teachers?

In small groups, assume the role of one of the case stakeholders. Write a statement/dialogue expressing this person's or group's hypothetical feelings and perspectives. Be prepared to act out your roles to the large group.

- ESL teacher
- content teacher
- Medha's mother
- school counselor/behavior specialist
- school nurse

### Surface Issues

What are the surface issues in this case? What is happening here from an untrained perspective? What underlying assumptions or beliefs feed into this perspective?

### Deep Issues

Discuss the real issues in the case. Try to categorize them in terms of language teaching curriculum and instruction.

### *Evidence-Based Solutions*

In groups, develop evidence-based solutions for each deep issue listed. Whenever possible, refer to a theory or principle of language learning and teaching to support your proposed solutions.

### *Teacher Thinking*

In what ways does this case influence and/or reinforce your beliefs and dispositions as a teacher? Consult the Further Resources section to help with theoretically informed solutions.

## III. POST-CASE PROBLEM SETS

### *Post-Case Analysis*

A. Categorize what you learned as:
   - teacher knowledge and praxis (e.g., content knowledge, curricular knowledge, pedagogical content knowledge and application)
   - teacher thinking (e.g., beliefs, problem-solving strategies, prioritizing objectives, values, professional ethics, attitudes)

B. List:
   - learning objectives that you discovered in the case
   - potential learning outcomes
   - implications for your pedagogical practices

C. The post-case problem sets introduce reactions from various perspectives. These quotes are from others who have read the cases for educational and pedagogical purposes. Read all of the quotes and then choose two about which to write a short response (put the quotes at the top of each response).  Use these questions as a guide:
   - What is the message the speaker is trying to convey? If possible, also explain why you chose the quote.
   - What examples can you think of that connect to the themes presented?
   - Can you relate the quote to a class discussion or to something you have read or experienced?

Quotes

1. "Medha needs to learn how to learn. Perhaps she has never been to school before kindergarten."
2. "The school should require teachers to make home visits so that the teacher can assess the exposure to home literacy practices in the home."
3. "The student has nothing wrong with her; she simply needs better glasses."
4. "This school needs to do less testing and more teaching."
5. "The mother does not seem to really understand school protocol. Why did she call the teacher last minute?"

D. Write a reflection describing a take-away from the case in terms of praxis. Make sure to develop an action plan to resolve the case. Consider these questions as guidelines:

- In what ways did the case discussion influence your thinking about the case?
- Did you change your original decision or did the discussion reaffirm your position?
- What points had you not considered prior to the case discussion?
- How might the information you gained from this case be applicable to your current instructional setting and/or future instructional settings?
- What did you learn?
- What are you inspired to learn more about?
- How did the themes discussed in class apply to your experience?

E. Discuss what theoretical basis there is for:

- the stakeholders' behavior in the case.
- the solutions you proposed.

## Further Reading and Resources

August, D., Carlo, M., Lively, T. J., McLaughlin, B., & Snow, C. (2006). Promoting the vocabulary growth of English learners. In T. A. Young & N. L. Hadaway (Eds.), *Supporting the literacy development of English learners* (pp. 96–112). Newark, DE: International Reading Association, Inc.

Brown, J. E., & Doolittle, J. (2008). *A cultural, linguistic and ecological framework for response to intervention with English language learners.* Tempe, AZ: National Center for Culturally Responsive Education Systems.

Calderón, M., August, D., Slavin, R., Durán, A. D., & Madden, N. (2005). Bringing words to life in classrooms with English language learners. In A. Hiebert & M. Kamil (Eds.), *Research and development on vocabulary.* Mahwah, NJ: Lawrence Erlbaum.

Klingner, J.K., & Artiles, A.J. (2003). Distinguishing English language learners from special education students. *Educational Leadership, 61*(2), 66–71.

Kovaleski, J. F. (2002). Best practices in operating pre-referral intervention teams. In J. G. A. Thomas (Ed.), *Best practices in school psychology IV* (pp. 645–655). Washington, DC: National Association of School Psychologists.

Ortiz, A. A. (1997). Learning disabilities occurring concomitantly with linguistic differences. *Journal of Learning Disabilities, 30*, 321–323.

Paradis, J., Genesee, F., & Crago, M.B. (2010). *Dual language development and disorders: A handbook on bilingualism and second language learning* (2nd ed.). Baltimore, MD: Brookes.

Shillady, A. (2014). Engaging families in diverse communities: Strategies from elementary school principals. *Young Children, 69*(4), 46–49. Retrieved from http://www.naeyc.org/yc/pastissues/2014/september

Shillady, A., & Charner, K. (2014). Engaging families: Partnering in meaningful ways. *Young Children, 69*(4), 6–7. Retrieved from http://www.naeyc.org/yc/pastissues/2014/september

# Chapter 3

# Cases in Secondary ESL/SEI/ TESOL

The cases in this chapter span a wide range of relevant topics in the education of secondary English learners in traditional ESL and sheltered content area settings. In Case 3.1, *Reddington High*, the teacher attempts to find effective strategies to promote literacy instruction for secondary English learners who, in addition to meeting academic goals, also struggle with the sociocultural stresses of living in a high-crime, low-socioeconomic community. In Case 3.2, *John Cassidy High*, the reader is asked to analyze the efficacy of a teacher's curricular design and instructional strategies in a sheltered English world literature classroom. In Case 3.3, *Rose Hall High*, the themes of motivation and language learning and culturally responsive curricula emerge in the description of the challenges confronting a high school ESL teacher.

This chapter is designed to encourage collaborative inquiry about important educational issues such as strategies for helping secondary English learners tackle complex texts; adopting culturally responsive dispositions and pedagogy and dispositions; designing content-based lessons that are relevant and meaningful via SIOP and PACE models; using varied grouping and scaffolding techniques and promoting higher-order thinking; creating curricula that promotes intrinsic or extrinsic learner motivation; and differentiating input, product, and process in multi-level classrooms.

# ▪▪▪▪▪▪▪▪▪▪▪▪▪▪▪▪ CASE 3.1 ▪▪▪▪▪▪▪▪▪▪▪▪▪▪▪▪

# Reddington High

Reddington High is an urban public school whose mission boasts an academic experience aimed to "help students gain essential skills for a future full of opportunity." Originally constructed and owned by a textile mill, the building was converted into a school in the early 1980s and the eerie, frigid ambience is reflective of that era. Only four miles to the northeast is an affluent school district whose teachers and principals have been praised in the news for their educational leadership and student academic success. The gaps in achievement and student retention between these two nearby districts is glaring. The town of Reddington has made slow changes during the past decade—but high dropout and unemployment rates and gang-related violence and crime still plague the community.

A beautiful welcome message at the entrance to the school is displayed in Spanish, Portuguese, and English. An international variety of flags hangs overhead on the ceiling. Two staff members and a police officer greet visitors as they pass through the metal detectors. The building has six floors, and the stairways are wide and unheated. Some of the windows in one stairway have been vandalized and remain broken. Only teachers and staff have access to the one, dreadfully slow elevator. The school library is physically large but feels empty; ten dated computers are available for student use. A girls' bathroom on one floor is littered with trash and has empty soap dispensers, one dim light barely illuminating the dank space, and cracked "mirrors" made from shined metal that reflect an image like the distorting mirrors one might find at a carnival. The staff restrooms are frequently without toilet paper or hand towels. The lockers that line the hallways are dented and marked, missing locks and in some cases, doors. According to school policy, teachers must stand outside of their classrooms between classes to act as vigilant monitors of any misconduct and violence.

The few decorations in Ms. Arlington's classroom are school posters with outdated education slogans that have been up for two decades. One displays in cursive "A Good Sentence…" and another has the steps of the writing process. Dust has accumulated along the windowsill, and gum lines the underside of the tables and chairs. The canvas curtains are always closed, covering four large windows. There are no desks, only tables. One side of the classroom is lined with a small bookshelf and filing cabinets, upon which there are numerous papers, binders, and miscellaneous objects. The bookshelf has roughly 100–200 books, mostly children's picture books and other children's series like *Diary of a Wimpy Kid*.

Ms. Arlington explains that her own daughter read these same books when she was at that literacy level; now her daughter is a sophomore in college. The front of the room has a chalkboard and two other spaces—one covered by what looks like a whiteboard (but is not), the other covered with brown paper, upon which Ms. Arlington posts index cards with vocabulary items. These cards are difficult to read from where the students sit and are not changed frequently.

Ms. Arlington works with two groups of students, each for two periods ESL 2 and ESL 3. Reddington High operates on block scheduling: Mondays and Thursdays are 60-minute periods, Tuesdays and Wednesdays are 70-minute periods, and Fridays are 45-minute periods and early dismissal at 12:45. Every student has an advisory period, which tends to be a free period, on Mondays and Thursdays in addition to classes. The ESL 2 class has 14 students and ESL 3 has 16. The numbers fluctuate frequently because students come and go; expulsions and drop-outs occur with surprising regularity.

An additional challenge is the disruptive noise coming from the two classrooms on either side. According to Ms. Arlington, "One classroom houses ESL 2, where many students do not speak any English and have not been acculturated to the expectations of appropriate classroom behavior. For the first few weeks of school, their class had no teacher, only a revolving door of substitutes. Once the school did hire a full-time teacher for the position, he was entirely ineffective and apparently unqualified, as he had never worked with LEP students before." According to that teacher's daily reports on the school-wide network used to report issues, he sometimes reported academic concerns, but they usually related to problematic behavior and troublesome students. Reportedly, students in the class were disrespectful of their teacher and would disregard his instructions and warnings.

Not too long ago, the ESL 2 class started reading a book called *Onion Tears* (Grade Levels 3–5). The students are now answering simple comprehension questions based on three pages. Reading is always done as a whole-class activity, never independently because, Ms. Arlington says, "They aren't there yet"—able to read in groups or by themselves. Typically, the lesson consists of one student reading out loud. On one particular day, the students read two pages in approximately 55 minutes. At the end of each paragraph, Ms. Arlington asks if there are any words students didn't comprehend, but she does not really check comprehension. About five minutes are spent discussing the meaning of "dried fish" because it turns into a discussion of how that implies something different for the students from Puerto Rico and those from the Dominican Republic. According to the teacher, the discussion is very loud, with every student wanting to add something, but it does not relate to the text or promote a greater understanding of it.

The next day Ms. Arlington asks the students to draw a picture that describes what they read. This is an idea from a recent workshop she attended. There are a lot of complaints coming from the students, and many are not even working. Asked about an alternative to the drawing that these students could do, Ms. Arlington exclaims: "Too bad. They have to." In the end, she adds, "This is why these professional development trainings are a waste of time. These professors have no idea of the reality in my classroom. All of this multiple modalities and multiple intelligence stuff sounds good in theory. As far as I am concerned, it has nothing to do with helping them focus on reading and writing development in academic English."

On another day, the students are berated for not signing the attendance list when the teacher was absent. Five out of 14 students have not signed the sheet or turned in work, so Ms. Arlington gives them zeroes. She then announces the new assignment is to write 20 present perfect sentences using words from the list of irregular past verbs and past participles; students should write 10 questions and 10 negative sentences. Before the students begin writing, she reviews the meanings of the verbs and gives one example sentence for each verb.

As the students work, there is a lot of commotion and off-task conversation. Most of the sentences produced demonstrate little or no understanding of the present perfect even though they have been studying the present perfect for more than a month. Many students have a lot of questions about the verbs, and their sentences reveal poor comprehension of when to use the present perfect and the vocabulary.

On another day, there is chaos. The focus is on one student, Milton. He speaks in Spanish with his classmates, but the teacher, who understands Spanish, investigates what has happened. Milton explains that two men jumped him and Ronaldo, another student in the class, on their way into school. Apparently the men had seen Ronaldo using his cell phone, so they pursued the boys, took the phone (with the threat of a gun in the waist of his pants), and beat Ronaldo, but Milton was not physically harmed. Ronaldo was taken to the hospital in an ambulance. This incident took place in front of the school building at 7:30 AM.

On another day, Ms. Arlington assigns a small project-based activity on the topic of the environment. Students are placed in pairs and assigned different factors causing damage, such as air pollution and deforestation. The whole class does research in the library. Assistance from the librarian or the teacher is not allowed. The teacher explains the assignment, tells the students when the project is due, gives them a list of some websites to consult, and leads them to the computers. One of the websites is National Geographic, and since most students recognize it, the majority of them go there first. One girl in particular, Marianna, whose partner is absent, is searching for facts on the website but cannot seem to type her topic, air pollution, correctly. She finds information featured on the screen quite sophisticated. Even when the material is explained to her, she has a difficult time comprehending seemingly simple concepts. The bell rings before she is able to print any information (each group is allowed to print one page of information) or get any help from her teacher.

In ESL 3, students have made little progress in six months. The group is reading *The Diary of Anne Frank*, and the disparities in students' reading ability are concerning. One student, Vera, is on page 80, while several of her classmates have not passed page 10. Another girl, Karen, does not understand what is happening in the book, and also does not have the slightest idea of the historical context. The students admit that they do not read outside of class because most of them work or simply don't care enough to do so. Ms. Arlington tells them that they "are never going to finish the book." She often comments on how slowly the students work and how little they accomplish.

Throughout the term, Ms. Arlington gives cumulative vocabulary tests to each class plus unit tests on the textbook they've used in the prior months. These tests can take up to two full class periods for some students to complete; many students simply choose not to respond to the final essay questions. In the last week of the ten-week term, both of Ms. Arlington's classes must take a mid-term exam that was created by the district to measure the progress of their literacy skills; the focus is not only on language skills. When Ms. Arlington sees the blank pages, she shrugs and shakes her head.

All the students are particularly resistant to the tests. During tests, they constantly ask questions.

"What does *proofread* mean?"

"I don't understand number 23."

"Ms. Arlington! What am I supposed to do on this one?"

In an attempt to maintain the validity of the tests and obtain untainted results, Ms. Arlington has decided not to answer any questions students when they are taking a test. As a result, the students are worried, or they haphazardly fill in answers.

When Ms. Arlington returns the graded tests and students are upset after seeing their grades, she asks, "Why didn't you just ask me?" There is, not surprisingly, an uproar in the class.

"We were afraid," says Lissette. Ms. Arlington doesn't seem to hear her.

Ms. Arlington continues, "Well, always ask me. I'll tell you if I can't tell you. But you should always ask me if you don't know something."

The students accept their grades. Ms. Arlington passes out the next test.

A couple of students in ESL 2 consistently arrive 10 or 15 minutes late. Pedro is from Guatemala and he wants to do a good job. Miguel, from the Dominican Republic, is a star baseball player. Pedro typically does very well in the class, but

Ms. Arlington is unforgiving about tardiness. On one of the days he comes in late, the class is taking a test, and Ms. Arlington will not let him take it. He doesn't argue; he just puts his head on his desk, embarrassed and defeated.

Miguel struggles immensely and will fail Ms. Arlington's class this marking term. His reading level is somewhere in the range of second or third grade. The teacher knows he should move down to ESL 1, but the administrators will not allow it. He needs a certain G.P.A. to be eligible for the baseball team. At the beginning of the week, Ms. Arlington intends to give him a "P" on his report card. Although the principal won't approve of it, this is the grade reserved for students who have been placed in the wrong class and cannot keep up with the work. However, when Miguel walks in late on Friday morning, she tells herself, "That's it. I'm failing him. And that will be the end of the baseball team for him." To others, she says, "I've had enough. He has to learn that he cannot come in late everyday. You know Maria? She used to come in late, but she made it her New Year's resolution to be on time. She's changed. He should be able to also. That's just too bad."

The principal says via the intercom that the school is now on "containment." Students are not to leave the classroom, to disregard all bells, and any students or faculty in the hallways are to get into the nearest classroom immediately. This is the standard procedure when someone has brought a gun to school. Everyone sits in the classroom for the next hour, until they get the "all-clear."

One student plays videos on his iPhone. Two others try to finish the test. One student sits quietly, staring into space, while another is listening to music so loud in his headphones that it can be heard across the room. Ms. Arlington sits at one of the computers in the back corner of the room.

Then comes the announcement that everyone can leave in five minutes when the bell rings. As the students trail out the door, a frustrated Ms. Arlington looks at her desk and wonders if she will ever be able to move this group forward with this curriculum and what she can do to get the students to think.

### ▪ Exhibit A: School Profile

Of the school's 1,349 students, 49 percent are Hispanic and 41 percent are African-American. According to district measures, 34 percent of the student population is considered to be LEP. The ELL demographic represents an array of learners whose families immigrated to the U.S. from Puerto Rico, El Salvador, the Dominican Republic, Cape Verde, Mexico, and Jamaica in search of a better life. Of the entire student population, 62 percent live below the poverty line. Many ELLs are expected to take care of younger siblings or help out with the household. About 28 percent of ELLs come from single mother households and, in some cases, while their mothers work multiple jobs, they are responsible for the household affairs. Most students commute to school by train or bus because no transportation is provided by the city.

Some ELLs did not attend school consistently back in their home country due to political or economic strife, so assessment and referral requires native-speaker staff support, which is not always available. The school offers TESOL classes for newcomers and once they are considered proficient, they can be mainstreamed into classes with native speakers.

## ■ Exhibit B: Description of Weekly Quizzes

All of the students have a list of irregular past tense verbs and past participles. Ms. Arlington passes out a quiz about past tense verbs or past participles that requires conjugating a base form verb or re-writing a list of statements as questions. The quiz takes up an entire 45-minute class period.

Another quiz is a list of 80 verbs to be conjugated along with statement-question changes on the back. Almost an entire 70-minute class period is taken up with this quiz; of 30 students in all, no more than four students earn a passing grade.

## I. Pre-Case Discussion Problems Sets

Complete the chart after reading the case.

| | |
|---|---|
| Facts | |
| Opinions | |
| Assumptions | |
| Theories referred or connected to (if any) | |
| Ambiguous language | |
| Criteria you used in analyzing the case (e.g., emotional vs. rational) | |
| Emerging options | |

Write a pre-case discussion decision paper. Include these points:

a. options for case resolution

b. criteria (a rational decision should always be made with a set of criteria)

c. analysis of options

d. recommendation (of the best choice among the options)

e. action plan

## II. CASE DISCUSSION QUESTIONS

### *Big-Picture Analysis*

Describe the sociocultural issues impacting the community within which Reddington High is embedded.

- How do these issues trickle into the classroom?
- What is your impression of the school culture?
- What do we know about the ELL curriculum? About students?

### *Stakeholders*

What do we know about Ms. Arlington? How would you define her philosophy of teaching? What is her relationship with her learners? What do we know about the learners in the classroom?

In small groups, assume the role of one of the case stakeholders. Write a statement/dialogue expressing this person's or group's hypothetical feelings and perspectives. Be prepared to act out your roles to the large group.

- administrators
- teachers
- parents
- students in the class

### *Surface Issues*

What are the surface issues in this case? What is happening here from an untrained perspective? What underlying assumptions or beliefs feed into this perspective?

## *Deep Issues*

Discuss the real issues in the case. Try to categorize them in terms of language teaching curriculum and instruction.

## *Evidence-Based Solutions*

In groups, develop evidence-based solutions for each deep issue listed. Whenever possible, refer to a theory or principle of language learning and teaching to support your proposed solutions.

# III. Post-Case Problem Sets

## *Post-Case Analysis*

A. Categorize what you learned as:

- teacher knowledge and praxis (e.g., content knowledge, curricular knowledge, pedagogical content knowledge and application)
- teacher thinking (e.g., beliefs, problem-solving strategies, prioritizing objectives, values, professional ethics, attitudes)

B. List:

- learning objectives that you discovered in the case
- potential learning outcomes
- implications for your pedagogical practices

C. The post-case problem sets introduce reactions from various perspectives. These quotes are from others who have read the cases for educational and pedagogical purposes. Read all of the quotes and then choose two about which to write a short response (put the quotes at the top of each response). Use these questions as a guide:

- What is the message the speaker is trying to convey? If possible, also explain why you chose the quote.
- What examples can you think of that connect to the themes presented?
- Can you relate the quote to a class discussion or to something you have read or experienced?

## Quotes

1. "Regretfully, it seems as though this teacher has the attitude that a lot of teachers have—'it's not me; it's them.' They believe that these students are failing because they do not care or want to learn the language, when really the system and teachers are failing them. This outlook leads to a dead end. This case has made me think a lot about teachers' attitudes and their impact on the learning environment. As teachers, we have to be willing accept some blame when things go wrong. We have to believe that our students can achieve."

2. "Ms. Arlington could be even more effective if she used the SIOP model and if she pre-taught rather than tutored her ELLs. It's easy to get into a lesson-planning/delivering routine (even a working one) that slowly but surely leads a good teacher away from successful lesson planning practices such as the ones endorsed by SIOP. In general, the use of some differentiated learning methods would be useful—her students are not engaged in appropriate or effective ways. There are obviously varying skill levels among the students. It is necessary to use not only varied methods of instruction but also to find out how these students' levels differ because this would open an understanding of what can be done in order to best use one's time instructing."

3. "To the teacher, assessment equals evaluation, and that equals test. She doesn't use assessment to measure progress—as there doesn't seem to be any. She doesn't have a variety of methods of assessment or even assess what she actually should have taught. Do all the ELL teachers in this school do the same thing? Maybe they could get together and come up with some assessments in common. That would help Ms. Arlington see beyond 90-minute grammar tests."

4. "Ms. Arlington needs to wake up and take a graduate class. Someone needs to inform her that the old kill-drill method is not an acceptable teaching approach. It has not been the manner of teaching for more than a decade. I hope that someone will tell her that meaningful and interactive lesson plans are not a thing of the future, but of the present! It is very depressing that Ms. Arlington is so stuck in her ways of "old-school" teaching. She is doing these students a serious disservice and is using a "banking method of education" that is completely disconnected from students' lives."

5. "One literacy activity she could use is the popcorn reading strategy, where students each read a short section of the material out loud but are selected at random. This helps students to be attentive so that they know what they're reading when they get called on. Choral reading is another method of whole-class out-loud reading. Partner and small-group reading is also a good technique to change things up, provided that students are well paired and have a few good questions to answer after the reading. They also need each to have a role (e.g., predictor, summarizer, etc.)."

D. Write a reflection describing a take-away from the case in terms of praxis. Make sure to develop an action plan to resolve the case. Consider these questions as guidelines:

- In what ways did the case discussion influence your thinking about the case?
- Did you change your original decision or did the discussion reaffirm your position?
- What points had you not considered prior to the case discussion?
- How might the information you gained from this case be applicable to your current instructional setting and/or future instructional settings?
- What did you learn?
- What are you inspired to learn more about?
- How did the themes discussed in class apply to your experience?

E. Discuss what theoretical basis there is for:

- the stakeholders' behavior in the case.
- the solutions you proposed.

## Further Reading and Resources

Bartolomé, L. (1994). Beyond the methods fetish: Toward a humanizing pedagogy. *Harvard Educational Review, 64*(2), 173–194.

Calderón, M. (2011). *Teaching reading and comprehension to English learners, K–5.* Bloomington, IN: Solution Tree Press.

DeCapua, A., & Marshall, H. W. (2011). *Breaking new ground: Teaching students with limited or interrupted formal education in U.S. secondary schools.* Ann Arbor: University of Michigan Press.

DeCapua, A., Smathers, W., & L. F. Tang. (2009). *Meeting the needs of students with limited or interrupted schooling: A guide for educators.* Ann Arbor: University of Michigan Press.

Fry, R. (2003). Hispanic youth dropping out of U.S. schools: Measuring the challenge. Retrieved from: http://pewhispanic.org/files/reports/19.pdf

Marshall, H.W., & DeCapua, A. (2013). *Making the transition to classroom success: Culturally responsive teaching for struggling language learners.* Ann Arbor: University of Michigan Press.

Peregoy, S. F., Boyle, O., & Peregoy, S. F. (2005). *Reading, writing, and learning in ESL: A resource book for K–12 teachers.* Boston: Pearson/Allyn and Bacon.

RanceRoney, J. (2009). Best practices for adolescent ELLs. *Educational Leadership, 66*(7), 32. doi: 167343011.

Snow, M.A., & Brinton, D. (2017). *The content-based classroom* (Second Ed.). Ann Arbor: University of Michigan Press.

Trumbull, E., & Pacheco, M. (2005). Culture, families, communities, and schools. In E. DeVaney & YJ. Noguchi (Eds.), *The teacher's guide to diversity: Building a knowledge base, Volume I: Human development, culture, and cognition* (pp. 123–131, 134–136). Providence, RI: Brown University.

Walqui, A. (2000). *Contextual factors of second language acquisition.* Washington, DC: CAL.

WIDA English Language Proficiency Standards (2007 and 2012). www.wida.us

Wright, W. E. (2010). *Foundations for teaching English language learners: Research, theory, policy, and practice.* Philadelphia: Caslon Publishing.

# ▪▪▪▪▪▪▪▪▪▪▪▪▪▪▪▪ CASE 3.2 ▪▪▪▪▪▪▪▪▪▪▪▪▪▪▪▪

# John Cassidy High

Before entering John Cassidy High School, the students encounter narrow pathways and busy construction workers because the school is still in the process of being remodeled. Once inside, the students are greeted by the main security officer on duty. Murals as well as glass cases of student artwork are displayed in the hallways of the first floor. When the bell rings, everybody walks over to their respective classrooms. After first period, the students attend a short 20-minute homeroom (for attendance and announcements). Homeroom period, with its mix of all the students, is the best way to get a look at the diverse student body. Some students spend that time listening to hip hop and working on their dance moves, others work on last-minute assignments for the next class or on homework for the next day. There seems to be a rare mixture of interactions between the two groups. However, the students respect each other's space, which reduces the possibility of conflicts.

Four flights up the main stairs is Ms. Yeras' Advanced SEI World Literature II class for sophomore ELLs. The goals and objectives for each week are written in bold and colorful writing on the chalkboard. The whiteboard shows the agenda and assignments for the class that day, which the teacher reviews at the beginning of class. Ms. Yeras expects students to come to class on time and prepared, so when the bell rings, students must be in their seats with their materials out on the desks. Most of the students are good about accomplishing this task, but even toward the end of the semester, there are some who enter the classroom late. The class consists of 14 boys with one girl. The majority speak Spanish, Portuguese, or Haitian Creole. During class, the students can be heard speaking their home language to their peers, especially if they need clarification.

The ELLs do not seem to fit well into the school population because they do not get many opportunities to be mainstreamed with their peers until junior year of high school. Some of the students are driven to improve their English language ability so they can master other academic skills, but the rest do not see a purpose to improving their English.

Ms. Yeras has a Portuguese background, and she has only been teaching SEI World Literature for a few years at John Cassidy High School. She admits it is a challenge to cater to the needs of the ELLs and has been thinking each year about making adjustments to her lessons to better meet their needs, but once the semester begins, it is a whirlwind and too difficult.

If there is enough time at the beginning of the class, Ms. Yeras likes to start off with a news activity. Every day, the students like to bring in the *Metro* newspaper, hoping Ms. Yeras will find an interesting article to discuss. Students appear to be a little more upbeat or motivated when they get to do this activity. The students seem to have a good response to this activity, especially during election years. They seemed to be aware of what was going on in the country, and they were eager to learn vocabulary words they could use in their conversations or writing on this topic. Unfortunately, some days there isn't time.

Ms. Yeras also tries to incorporate grammar warm-ups, and this semester she is spending time on phrasal verbs. Students are given about 20 minutes to complete a worksheet with phrasal verbs. Each day, a new phrasal verb is taught, and the teacher tries to give a quiz to follow up on the lesson. She does not explain the purpose of these grammar activities, and even though the quizzes are only supposed to take about ten minutes, she is often lenient about giving the students as much as 20 to 25 minutes. The anxiety of the students can be seen as they frantically study for the quiz for whatever little time they have before the bell rings for class. Many of the students ask the teacher to review the lesson.

In another lesson, the rest of the class time is dedicated to reading and comprehending the assigned literature. This term, the novel is *Things Fall Apart*, and even though the teacher assigns the reading for homework, every chapter of the book is read and dissected during the class. Since Ms. Yeras teaches a literature class, the students are expected to approach literature with not just a literal but also a critical eye. Ms. Yeras likes to do a pre-reading activity before they start a book. Most of the time, she tries to do group presentation projects, where the students research the cultural or historical setting of the novel. The students can thus get a feel for the plot and characters of this novel. Ms. Yeras admits that she is not a big fan of group projects: She feels her students are having trouble understanding the idea of teamwork, but she sees the need to incorporate it somehow because other classes require group activities or assignments. When she assigned different African tribes to students to research before they read *Things Fall Apart*, only one group seemed to get the point of cooperative learning and completed the task. Every group was in charge of researching the cultural, political, and social aspects of the tribal group they were assigned, and every group member was responsible for a particular task. Group A succeeded because it had a leader, Derek. Although each student had separate roles and responsibilities, such as researching or typing the report, Derek facilitated the group's progress. In addition, they made decisions together, especially when they were working on the graphic design portion of the assignment. Other groups had stubborn members like Christian, who made sure they were responsible only for the minimal amount of work, and they did not want to participate after they finished their portion of the project. Ms. Yeras lost patience with the attitude of students like Christian because they caused argu-ments among the group members. So, she just let those students do the minimal amount of work, which meant that the other students had to do more work to fin-ish the group project presentation. However, since there are typically about four to five students in each group, the students are able to divide the roles based on their talents or their best learning style. Ms. Yeras has had the most success with her "see, think, wonder" activity, which is similar to a KWL chart: A cover of the book is blown up into a PowerPoint, and the students write down the images they see, what they think the images mean, and what they wonder about. Students seem to be the most engaged or active during this activity.

Every day, Ms. Yeras asks the students to summarize what they went over in the last class, and they are to predict, occasionally in their journals, what they believe will occur in the next chapter of the book. Then, the teacher reads the entire chapter aloud to the students for the rest of the class, and the students are expected just to follow along. At this time, most of the students are focused on the reading, but there a few students like Jason, who pretends to be following but is actually doodling. Ms. Yeras does not seem to take note of these students as she contin-ues to read the chapter. Sometimes, she will stop in the middle of her reading to go over any unknown vocabulary words and significant events occurring in the chapter. The structure of the discussions is always the same, and usually the same students end up participating. Toward the end of class, she once again reviews what has occurred in the novel up to the chapter they read, and sometimes they are assigned comprehension questions relating to the chapter read for homework. Rarely does she give a creative assignment for homework, like the time she had the students draw the setting of the novel based on the description in the text. Students were most likely to finish this assignment than take the time to answer the comprehension questions in their reading packet. Occasionally, the teacher will throw in some open response questions regarding the novel because they have to practice their reader response skill for the state-mandated assessment in March. This is the standard approach for the literature portion of the classroom most of the days, and the boredom of this routine is apparent in the expressions of the students throughout the classroom period. Even the teacher's energy seems to be drained after reading just one chapter of the novel. There is a good ten minutes to utilize before the class period is over, but the teacher lets her students get ready to leave. Only some students will utilize this time to work on their comprehension questions before class ends, while the other students can be seen filling out the questions for class the next day.

Most of the time Ms. Yeras has to stress that the homework assignments are for a grade so the students have at least some motivation to take the comprehension questions seriously. This also activates participation in class with the discussion of the comprehension questions. Other than collecting the homework or discussing the comprehension questions the teacher does not have a form of assessing their comprehension of the material and participation in class. Most of the discussions are between the teacher and the students, and opportunities when the students are interacting with each other are rare.

### ▌ Exhibit A: School Overview

John Cassidy High School enrolls 1,835 students in Grades 9–12. Situated within a gateway city for immigrants, the John Cassidy Public High School District serves a multilingual, multiethnic student population in an urban educational context. More than 44 percent of students report speaking a language other than English at home, reflecting a linguistic and cultural diversity and richness characteristic of a large urban city.

The school's administrators and teachers try to offer a learning environment conducive to the academic, social, and civic aspect of a student's life. The learning environment should enable students to develop critical-thinking skills, interpersonal skills, and the ability to take responsibility for their behavior. The International Program was specifically established to meet these needs of English language learners. Students who take part in the International Program are assisted in their sequence of intensive English language courses with a supplementary curriculum and facilitation in their native language when necessary. The students will not only develop academic skills required to be mainstreamed into regular classrooms but will also be exposed to different aspects of American culture. In terms of resources, the Amistad Federal Grant provides funds to the Bilingual and Language Acquisition Department in order to offer English language learners opportunities to receive instruction for statewide standardized tests. The fund covers ESL as well as computer literacy classes for families, and there are monthly forums held for families to be informed about issues regarding immigration and adolescent development.

### ▌ Exhibit B: ELL Demographic Data

About 22 home languages are represented among current ELLs in the school. The following languages are spoken by the 1,098 ELLs in the district: Spanish (6.5 percent), Chinese (9.8 percent), Portuguese (6.2 percent), French/Hatian Creole (6.6 percent), Vietnamese (3.9 percent), as well as Albanian, Amharic, Arabic, Cape Verdean, Filipino, Gujarati, Hindi, Khmer, Luganda, Nepali, Pashtu,

Russian, Somali, Tamil, Thai, Tibetan, and Urdu. About 16 percent of the student population is considered LEP. Of all current ELLs at the middle school level, 13.4 percent are in SEI classrooms and 47.6 percent are in SEI 2 classrooms.

According to socioeconomic data, 95 percent of ELLs live at or below the poverty line and most ELLs receive free or reduced lunch. About 97 percent of ELLs enrolled in the schools are first-generation immigrants. Many of these students have had interrupted formal schooling experiences and some students are not literate in their first language. The district data indicate that only 76 percent of ELLs graduate and many are categorized as academically "at risk."

## I. PRE-CASE DISCUSSION PROBLEMS SETS

Complete the chart after reading the case.

| | |
|---|---|
| Facts | |
| Opinions | |
| Assumptions | |
| Theories referred or connected to (if any) | |
| Ambiguous language | |
| Criteria you used in analyzing the case (e.g., emotional vs. rational) | |
| Emerging options | |

Write a pre-case discussion decision paper. Include these points:

a. options for case resolution

b. criteria (a rational decision should always be made with a set of criteria)

c. analysis of options

d. recommendation (of the best choice among the options)

e. action plan

## II. CASE DISCUSSION QUESTIONS

### Big-Picture Analysis

Describe the context of the case.

- school background and learning environment
- ELL student demographic information
- ELL student schoolwide support system

### Stakeholders

In small groups, assume the role of one of the case stakeholders. Write a statement/dialogue expressing this person's or group's hypothetical feelings and perspectives. Be prepared to act out your roles to the large group.

- Ms. Yeras
- students in her class
- administrative observer

### Surface Issues

What are the surface issues in this case? What is happening here from an untrained perspective? What underlying assumptions or beliefs feed into this perspective?

### Deep Issues

Discuss the real issues in the case. Try to categorize them in terms of language teaching curriculum and instruction.

## *Evidence-Based Solutions*

In groups, develop evidence-based solutions for each deep issue listed. Whenever possible, refer to a theory or principle of language learning and teaching to support your proposed solutions.

## *Teacher Thinking*

In what ways does this case influence and/or reinforce your beliefs and dispositions as a teacher? Consult the Further Resources section to help with theoretically informed solutions.

## III. POST-CASE PROBLEM SETS

### *Post-Case Analysis*

A. Categorize what you learned as:
- teacher knowledge and praxis (e.g., content knowledge, curricular knowledge, pedagogical content knowledge and application)
- teacher thinking (e.g., beliefs, problem-solving strategies, prioritizing objectives, values, professional ethics, attitudes)

B. List:
- learning objectives that you discovered in the case
- potential learning outcomes
- implications for your pedagogical practices

C. The post-case problem sets introduce reactions from various perspectives. These quotes are from others who have read the cases for educational and pedagogical purposes. Read all of the quotes and then choose two about which to write a short response (put the quotes at the top of each response). Use these questions as a guide:
- What is the message the speaker is trying to convey? If possible, also explain why you chose the quote.
- What examples can you think of that connect to the themes presented?
- Can you relate the quote to a class discussion or to something you have read or experienced?

Quotes

1. "At first I thought that the school environment was the most difficult and challenging thing about Ms. Yeras' situation. On closer inspection, the most effective means of improving her English literature class will be implementing new instructional strategies in the classroom. Teachers rarely examine their own teaching to make sure they are using up-to-date strategies."

2. "The teacher's students seem to need an attitude adjustment because they do not seem to care enough about school to come on time and come prepared. In addition, some of the students seem to refuse to do the work either because they are lazy or bored."

3. "It is great that she uses collaborative group work for completing assignments. However, done improperly those can be disastrous. Language teachers need to guide and monitor group work in order for it to be effective."

4. "We have to find ways to weave in culture into the curriculum and design lessons that are sensitive to and celebratory of students' cultural and linguistic diversity."

5. "Is this really an SEI classroom? What is the purpose of an SEI classroom? It does not seem like the lessons are aligned with any grade-level content."

D. Write a reflection describing a take-away from the case in terms of praxis. Make sure to develop an action plan to resolve the case. Consider these questions as guidelines:

- In what ways did the case discussion influence your thinking about the case?
- Did you change your original decision or did the discussion reaffirm your position?
- What points had you not considered prior to the case discussion?
- How might the information you gained from this case be applicable to your current instructional setting and/or future instructional settings?
- What did you learn?
- What are you inspired to learn more about?
- How did the themes discussed in class apply to your experience?

E. Discuss what theoretical basis there is for:

- the stakeholders' behavior in the case.
- the solutions you proposed.

## Further Reading and Resources

Bartolomé, L. (1994). Beyond the methods fetish: Toward a humanizing pedagogy. *Harvard Educational Review, 64*(2), 173–194.

Beck, I., McKeown, M., & Kucan, L. (2002). *Bringing words to life: Robust vocabulary instruction.* New York: The Gilford Press. www.fcoe.net/ela/pdf/Vocabulary/beck8.pdf

Brisk, M.E., Horan, D.A., & MacDonald, E. (2008). A scaffolded approach to learning to write. In L.S. Verplaetse & N. Migliacci (Eds.). *Inclusive pedagogy for English language learners: A handbook of research-informed practices.* Mahwah, NJ: Lawrence Erlbaum.

Coleman, R., & Goldenberg, C. (2010). What does research say about effective practices for ELLs? *Kappa Delta Pi Record, 46*(2), 60–65.

Cummins, J. (2002). Foreword. In P. Gibbons (Ed.), *Scaffolding language, scaffolding learning: Teaching second language learners in the mainstream classroom.* Portsmouth, NH: Heinemann.

DeCapua, A., & Marshall, H. W. (2011). *Breaking new ground: Teaching students with limited or interrupted formal education in U.S. secondary schools.* Ann Arbor: University of Michigan Press.

DeCapua, A., Smathers, W., & L. F. Tang. (2009). *Meeting the needs of students with limited or interrupted schooling: A guide for educators.* Ann Arbor: University of Michigan Press.

Donnelly, W.B., & Roe, C.J. (2010). Using sentence frames to develop academic vocabulary for English learners. *The Reading Teacher, 64*(2), 1–5.

Echevarria, J., Vogt, M.E., & Short, D.J. (2013). *Making content comprehensible for English learners: The SIOP Model* (4th Ed.). Boston: Pearson.

Gottlieb, M. (2006). *Assessing English language learners: Bridges from language proficiency to academic achievement.* Thousand Oaks, CA: Corwin Press.

Marshall, H.W., & DeCapua, A. (2013). *Making the transition to classroom success: Culturally responsive teaching for struggling language learners.* Ann Arbor: University of Michigan Press.

O'Day, J. (2009). Good instruction is good for everyone or is it? English language learners in a balanced literacy approach. *Journal of Education for Students Placed at Risk, 14*(1), 97–119.

Short D., & Echevarria, J. (2005). Teacher skills to support English language learners. *Educating Language Learners, 62*(4), 8–13.

## ▪▪▪▪▪▪▪▪▪▪▪▪▪▪▪ CASE 3.3 ▪▪▪▪▪▪▪▪▪▪▪▪▪▪▪
# Rose Hall High

In an ESL 2 classroom at the Rose Hall High School, the problem of students neglecting their homework has become insidious. Rose Hall has changed locations seven times and is currently situated in an old office building. The architecture is more industrial than educational, with surfaces of concrete and metal that amplify sound. The building is five stories high and mostly painted in forest green, Rose Hall's school color.

Once an extremely prestigious institution, Rose Hall is currently an under-performing school that has consistently failed to meet Adequate Yearly Progress under No Child Left Behind standards. The school is facing closure if it does not improve quickly, which has led to major reform. The headmaster is under enormous pressure to improve Rose Hall's standing, and this pressure is felt throughout the faculty and administration.

The ESL 2 class that is having trouble with homework takes place during the first two periods every day. As there are only six periods in a school day, nearly half of the students' academic life at Rose Hall takes place in this classroom. Each double class period is 100, 120, or 140 minutes, depending on the day. The classroom is on the fifth floor, and would have a view of the neighborhood and surrounding hills were the shades not perpetually drawn to fend off the sunlight that adds heat to the already too-warm top floor. There is one shelving unit full of books (the "Library"); the rest of the materials (dictionaries, thesauri, textbooks, fiction, etc.) are stored in cardboard boxes or padlocked cupboards. The yellowish walls are mostly bare, but there are a few items posted: magazine images of sports stars, a wood board for the weekly vocabulary words, a couple of maps, and a few small but cheerful posters about the writing process. Student work was recently displayed on one of the bulletin boards for a Parent Open House, and the students expressed enthusiasm and excitement to see their work exhibited.

The classroom doesn't have desks, but tables arranged end-to-end in a rectangle that includes the teacher's desk at the front. The intention is to encourage students' oral participation and a sense of classroom community. The focus is nonetheless on the teacher, with the chalkboard and teacher's desk at the front of the room, as well as a whiteboard that displays the day's objectives and the homework assignments.

The teacher, Ms. Widener, is a woman who speaks Spanish fluently and does not hesitate to offer students support in their native language. She has good rapport with the students and the need for disciplinary measures is uncommon. She plans the weekly agenda jointly with another ESL 2 teacher, Ms. Jordan. They share ideas and rely on each other to gauge progress and pacing.

The class consists of eleven boys and two girls, all of whom are native Spanish speakers. They are originally from many different places, including the Dominican Republic, Guatemala, Colombia, Honduras, and Puerto Rico, and they exhibit a wide range of English language abilities. There is also a plethora of personality types that often leads to an uneven distribution of class participation, as is the case in most classrooms. Most students are at a low-intermediate to intermediate level, with strong listening comprehension in English, but a preference for speaking Spanish unless they are prompted to practice their English. At least two students did not pass the class last year and are taking it for a second time, and these students in particular show little motivation to do their homework (perhaps because none of the material is new to them).

There is generally a positive atmosphere in the classroom, and the students tend to participate actively. On the whole, they seem genuinely motivated to learn English, and many students will practice orally during class, using new vocabulary and grammatical structures in new sentences. The problem is that, despite being motivated in class and there being a strong student-teacher rapport, the students rarely complete work outside the classroom, even when the assignments are very short and require very little thought. It is a strange phenomenon for students to work so diligently during class time, yet be so reticent to complete homework. Many of the students even attend an afterschool homework program, but it does not seem to yield any results. Simple assignments like copying vocabulary words and their definitions onto index cards are often not completed, and students appear unfazed by the row of zeros developing in Ms. Widener's grade book.

There is, of course, plenty of variation from one student to the next regarding homework completion. Some students often do homework assignments and do them well, but the majority complete assignments sporadically and turn in work of unpredictable quality. A few students face failure in this class if their homework habits do not change.

The most puzzling homework incident occurred on a Thursday one November. One student, Gloria, is a mother. Ms. Widener says that, because of Gloria's child's needs, Gloria is often absent from class and therefore has trouble keeping up with the work, even though she is a strong student who performs well on the assignments she is able to complete. On this particular day, Gloria had been absent the previous day. As Ms. Widener circled the room checking students' homework, Gloria called out in English, "Miss, you have to give me a break." Ms. Widener continued circulating, and when she arrived in front of Gloria, and saw that the homework was not completed, she explained the school policy that students who miss school need to come in before or after school to get their assignments and catch up on the work missed. The conversation switched to Spanish, and Gloria retorted that this wasn't fair. When Ms. Widener did not relent, Gloria became frustrated and angry. *"Me voy,"* she announced in a soft voice that was full of emotion, "I'm leaving." Ms. Widener calmly continued checking homework, and Gloria, not quite sure of her next move, slowly put on her coat. She stood resolute and announced again loudly and clearly, challenging Ms. Widener without looking at her, *"Me voy."* Ms. Widener turned to her slowly and said, in English, "Where will you go?" The response was, *"No sé, pero me voy."* Before Ms. Widener could say anything, Rubén, who sat next to Gloria, quickly and purposefully swept Gloria's backpack out of her reach. He passed it to the next boy at the table, who also passed it on. The backpack floated further and further from Gloria, handled by each student as though it were something precious and almost fragile, until it reached the end of the table and was hidden from view. Rubén stood up next to Gloria and gently guided her into his seat so she would be surrounded, protected, by the boys on either side. For a moment there wasn't a sound in the room. Then Ms. Widener spoke, "Isn't that nice? Your friends are taking care of you." Then she began the lesson.

At lunch, Ms. Widener talked to her fellow teacher, Ms. Jordan, about her problems getting this class to do their work outside of school. Ms. Jordan's advice was to prompt a discussion with the class to find out why completion of homework was an issue. Ms. Widener was afraid of the Pandora's box that this question might open up, but because she had no other solution in mind, she took her friend's advice. The next day, she designed a roundtable discussion asking students to discuss why homework is important and what obstacles are preventing their completion of it. She learned that there are many factors contributing to their inadequate homework performance.

"Ms.," said Mario, "I have to work at my father's bakery after school until 10 PM. When I get home I am so tired."

Another student, Julio, explained, "Ms. Widener, I have to watch my little brother and sister all afternoon and they are only 10 and 5. My mother works two shifts and I cannot get a chance to focus on the work."

Some other students said they held afterschool jobs, and at least one student was working full time. All of these students are first-generation immigrants who may still be adjusting to life in a new culture and environment.

Ms. Widener told the students that, although she better understood the obstacles they faced, they must be adults and learn how to manage their time and do the homework, or else they would be at risk of failing.

Ms. Widener shared this with Ms. Jordan at lunch the next day: "There is also an absence of peer pressure to do the homework, since the majority of students do not complete assignments. It may be that students feel it is impossible for the teacher to fail all of them for not doing their homework, and are therefore comfortable not doing the assignments."

Ms. Jordan replied, "Although the students' failure to do their homework is troubling, it seems to me that there is another reason, solidarity. Students support each other, and want to succeed *together*, as is apparent in the episode involving Gloria. Perhaps you can harness that feeling to help them avoid failure."

## ■ Exhibit A: School Demographics

There are currently 900 students enrolled at Rose Hall, down from 1,100 the previous year, in an effort to reduce class size and improve the quality of education. The current racial breakdown is 47 percent Hispanic, 47 percent African-American, 2 percent Caucasian, and 4 percent other. Students are divided into Small Learning Communities, which are located on different floors. This means that students do not have to travel up and down the stairs between classes, except to attend lunch and physical education.

## ■ Exhibit B: ESL Program Structure

Students who demonstrate LEP are placed in self-contained classrooms where they work on the English skills that will eventually allow them to transition into the general education classroom. There are three levels of ESL offered, and students take a placement test to determine which level is appropriate for them. These placements are sometimes adjusted, so students who perform well in ESL 2 can be promoted to an ESL 3 class during the first few weeks of school.

## I. Pre-Case Discussion Problems Sets

Complete the chart after reading the case.

| | |
|---|---|
| Facts | |
| Opinions | |
| Assumptions | |
| Theories referred or connected to (if any) | |
| Ambiguous language | |
| Criteria you used in analyzing the case (e.g., emotional vs. rational) | |
| Emerging options | |

Write a pre-case discussion decision paper. Include these points:

a. options for case resolution

b. criteria (a rational decision should always be made with a set of criteria)

c. analysis of options

d. recommendation (of the best choice among the options)

e. action plan

## II. CASE DISCUSSION QUESTIONS

### Big-Picture Analysis

Describe the context of the case.

- policy context: Adequate Yearly Progress
- curricular context: self-contained ESL class
- teaching and learning environment and climate at the Rose Hall High
- student demographics

### Stakeholders

In small groups, assume the role of one of the case stakeholders. Write a statement/dialogue expressing this person's or group's hypothetical feelings and perspectives. Be prepared to act out your roles to the large group.

- Ms. Widener
- Ms. Jordan
- Gloria
- Mario
- other students
- parents/guardians of students

### Surface Issues

What are the surface issues in this case? What is happening here from an untrained perspective? What underlying assumptions or beliefs feed into this perspective?

### *Deep Issues*

Discuss the real issues in the case. Try to categorize them in terms of language teaching curriculum and instruction.

### *Evidence-Based Solutions*

In groups, develop evidence-based solutions for each deep issue listed. Whenever possible, refer to a theory or principle of language learning and teaching to support your proposed solutions.

### *Teacher Thinking*

In what ways does this case influence and/or reinforce your beliefs and dispositions as a teacher? Consult the Further Resources section to help with theoretically informed solutions.

## III. POST-CASE PROBLEM SETS

### *Post-Case Analysis*

    A. Categorize what you learned as:
- teacher knowledge and praxis (e.g., content knowledge, curricular knowledge, pedagogical content knowledge and application)
- teacher thinking (e.g., beliefs, problem-solving strategies, prioritizing objectives, values, professional ethics, attitudes)

    B. List:
- learning objectives that you discovered in the case
- potential learning outcomes
- implications for your pedagogical practices

C. The post-case problem sets introduce reactions from various perspectives. These quotes are from others who have read the cases for educational and pedagogical purposes. Read all of the quotes and then choose two about which to write a short response (put the quotes at the top of each response). Use these questions as a guide:

- What is the message the speaker is trying to convey? If possible, also explain why you chose the quote.
- What examples can you think of that connect to the themes presented?
- Can you relate the quote to a class discussion or to something you have read or experienced?

Quotes

1. "The teacher needs to have a more flexible mindset about homework. She has to adapt to the needs of the students in the room. Perhaps the homework has no value or obvious purpose for the students."

2. "If we want to prepare these students for success in general education classes, we have to hold them to high standards and expectations. Homework is an essential aspect of learning and the teacher is doing a great job with a 'no excuses' attitude. In the end, the students need to know that incomplete homework will impact their grades. We can't cater to their needs, even though they have a lot of stresses. So do we all. It's called life, and they have got to get with the program."

3. "This teacher may need to create assignments that are functional or practical given the age and maturity level of these students."

4. "With such a wide range of learners in the room, it must be a challenge for the teacher to meet all of their needs. Sometimes it is just impossible to reach them all, and you have to just teach to the middle."

5. "Even though this is a self-contained ESL classroom, perhaps the teacher should follow a theme-based curriculum to generate increased student interest."

D. Write a reflection describing a take-away from the case in terms of praxis. Make sure to develop an action plan to resolve the case. Consider these questions as guidelines:

- In what ways did the case discussion influence your thinking about the case?
- Did you change your original decision or did the discussion reaffirm your position?
- What points had you not considered prior to the case discussion?
- How might the information you gained from this case be applicable to your current instructional setting and/or future instructional settings?
- What did you learn?
- What are you inspired to learn more about?
- How did the themes discussed in class apply to your experience?

E. Discuss what theoretical basis there is for:

- the stakeholders' behavior in the case.
- the solutions you proposed.

## Further Reading and Resources

Bernaus, M., & Gardner, R. C. (2008). Teacher motivation strategies, student perceptions, student motivation, and English achievement. *The Modern Language Journal, 92*(3), 387–401.

DeCapua, A., & Marshall, H. W. (2011). *Breaking new ground: Teaching students with limited or interrupted formal education in U.S. secondary schools.* Ann Arbor: University of Michigan Press.

DeCapua, A., Smathers, W., & L. F. Tang. (2009). *Meeting the needs of students with limited or interrupted schooling: A guide for educators.* Ann Arbor: University of Michigan Press.

Dörnyei, Z. (2009). The L2 motivational self system. In Z. Dörnyei & E. Ushioda (Eds.), *Motivation, language identity and the L2 self* (pp. 9–42). Bristol, England: Multilingual Matters.

Lee, J.S. (2010). Culturally relevant pedagogy for immigrant children and English language learners. In C. Faldis & G. Valdes (Eds.), *The yearbook of the national society for the study of education* (pp. 453–473). New York: Teachers College Press.

Lightbown, P. M., & Spada N. (2001). Factors affecting second language learning. In C.N. Candlin & N. Mercer (Eds.), *English language teaching in its social context* (pp. 28–43). London: Routledge.

Marshall, H.W., & DeCapua, A. (2013). *Making the transition to classroom success: Culturally responsive teaching for struggling language learners.* Ann Arbor: University of Michigan Press.

# Chapter 4

# Cases in Modern
# Foreign Language

The cases in this chapter cover challenging themes that confront educators in the context of modern foreign language instruction. The teacher in Case 4.1, *Oxford High*, Ms. Campbell, clearly has a preference for teaching her Honors Spanish classes and dislikes teaching the ironically labeled "College Preparatory Class" where students vary widely in ability and, to her mind, have no motivation or intention of pursuing language any further than the required minimum for graduation. She is very concerned with classroom management difficulties she encounters with this group of learners. In Case 4.2, *Charles Watson High*, the reader is introduced to a French Level 3 teacher who does not understand the cause of the consistent lack of student participation during activities related to a French video series. She needs to find effective strategies for maximizing listening comprehension and student interest. Case 4.3, *Descartes Immersion School*, documents the obstacles encountered by a high school French instructor at an elite high school as he struggles to promote oral language proficiency and sustain the interest of a group of primarily Haitian fourth-year students, who have a lower socioeconomic status. The teacher's "dilemma" from his perspective centers around this group's lack of motivation and seeming reluctance to speak the target language in class.

This chapter encourages critical reflection and dialogue on a range of current and enduring issues in the field of modern foreign language instruction, such as designing contextualized language learning and teaching experiences through content-based or task-based teaching and learning approaches; incorporating evidenced-based strategies for supporting the development of integrated skills (reading, writing, listening, and speaking); infusing culture and students' cultural backgrounds into the foreign language curriculum; constructing standards-based lessons (e.g., ACTFL standards and 5 Cs of foreign language instruction); incorporating varied and authentic language learning materials; differentiating foreign language instruction and curriculum based on students' levels and interests; maintaining rigor and high standards through scaffolding; and using ongoing formative and summative assessments.

■■■■■■■■■■■■■■■■■■ CASE 4.1 ■■■■■■■■■■■■■■■■

# Oxford High

Ms. Young enters the room and leans against the back counter. This is how Ms. Campbell knows that the third period is starting. Ms. Young is a teacher of Chinese heritage who was assigned as an aide "to help with classroom management." This class is a Level 2 college preparatory Spanish class with 18 students, most of whom come from working class families.

Approximately 1,802 students attend Oxford High in a city in the midwestern part of the U.S. The school is divided into four learning communities, or LCs, named Learning Community O, Learning Community C, Learning Community R, and Learning Community S. Each LC has between 400 and 450 students. These communities are supposed to give students a small-school feel. The students go to school with the same peers and have the same teachers for the core classes in the learning community. However, this structure appears to create additional levels of bureaucracy: It produces more paperwork and seems to hinders communication between schools and departments. For example, a student from first period who needs tutoring needs to go the tutoring center to fill out a form and then take it back to the teacher of first period for signing. If the tutoring coordinator does not have a tutor available and therefore does not know what to do, the student is sent back to the teacher. This creates frustration because the teacher believes it is the responsibility of the tutoring center to find tutors for students who need them. The student will be sent back to the tutoring center.

The students at Oxford are required to take four years of English, four years of history, three years of math and science, and two years of a foreign language to meet graduation requirements. Teachers are usually assigned a variety of levels, both honors and college preparatory. Levels 4 and 5 are not distinguished as honors or college preparatory since it is generally thought that students who continue on to those levels "usually want to be there." A Spanish teacher might teach a Level 4, a Level 1, and an Honors 2 class. It would be rare to have three Honors 3 classes. Ms. Campbell says that most of the teachers like to teach honors and upper-level classes because the students are more motivated. Therefore, everyone teaches a variety of courses, except in the rare cases where teachers prefer to teach only Levels 1 and 2.

Level 1 is not divided into honors and college prep and some Level 1 classes are designated for heritage speakers, which include students of all language abilities. Ms. Campbell, explains that "you'll get kids in a Level 1 class who are taking it again because they failed it but don't want to work because they think they know it already. But they really don't." Then there will be the students who are taking the class for the first time and really want to learn the material. It is difficult to teach the material but then have to re-teach because half of the class cannot grasp it.

Oxford High uses a semester schedule. A student might take Level 1 of a language the first semester as a freshman and then not take Level 2 until the second semester as a sophomore. However, the Level 2 class will also include students who are fresh out of Level 1.

When it comes to language learning, the students at Oxford are placed into two distinct groups: those who take honors classes and those who take college preparatory classes. The honors students are educationally ambitious; they value learning, progression, and competition. Their focus is on getting into a good college. Strangely enough, the students in the classes entitled "college preparatory" seem to be focused on education. For them, school and classes are places where they socialize with their friends and are seen. Their focus seems to be on immediate pleasure and satisfaction. Among the college-prep students, there are two categories: those eager to learn and do well, albeit if only for a grade, and those who are indifferent to poor marks and learning.

Back in the third period class, Ms. Campbell begins the lesson. It takes 10 minutes for the noise and interaction to dissipate to some chatter, silent smirking, and texting. Ms. Young's presence at the back of the room appears to have no effect on any of this. Ms. Campbell sticks to the prescribed schedule of classroom activities: attendance and homework, the warm-up, followed by verb drills, learning goals, instruction, and summary. Ms. Campbell says that "they [administration] really want[s] us to follow the schedule for classroom management purposes." Ms. Young is supposed to help in this regard but, according to Ms. Campbell, "She can't do much because she doesn't know the language." Indeed, the students seem to completely ignore Ms. Young. The teacher begins to collect the homework, which most of the students don't have, while they complete a warm-up activity of conjugating a verb in a list of sentences in the preterit tense. This is the point when the students are the quietest. During a transition, they talk, even to other students across the room. Most of the talk is criticism of what they are being asked to do.

Ms. Campbell next begins the instruction, which today is "train station" vocabulary. She uses an interactive PowerPoint, standing at the projector stand where the computer and controls are housed. The students are separated from the projector screen by the stand and a misplaced counter. Coco is sleeping with her head on the desk between her arms. Bart is throwing paper airplanes and other objects at another classmate. He is slyly dodging Ms. Campbell's gaze. Leticia is discreetly sending text messages. A few students appear to be copying the vocabulary into their notes. Ms. Young seems to be aware of everything going on, including Bart's aviation practice, but she takes no action. After more students begin talking and the noise level rises, Ms. Campbell remarks, "You need this in your notes because it's going to be on the test. I'm just trying to help you." The students quiet down somewhat. Finally, the third period ends and the students rambunctiously head off to lunch.

### ■ Exhibit A: School Profile

Oxford is a large high school in a city that is home to a few prestigious universities. Many of the students who attend Oxford come from families of professors, researchers, and other intellectually oriented professions. The city is home to peoples of different ethnicities, beliefs and backgrounds, but the inhabitants fall into only one of two socioeconomic statuses. The city of Oxford eliminated rent control in the past year, which led to the flight of the middle class. Those who can afford to stay are typically from the wealthy intellectual elite. The other group of people, who are mostly immigrants and African-Americans, are confined to a dense neighborhood of crowded three-family housing. Rent does not increase sharply or skyrocket in these areas, as there is no demand to live there. The second major group of students who attend Oxford come from this background.

### ■ Exhibit B: An Incident

The previous week, a student was behaving a little strangely. Chuck kept drinking grape juice out of a bottle. At one point in the class he spilled some, and Ms. Campbell escorted him to the dean. Later she commented, "I smelled wine when Chuck spilled it, so I took him to the dean."

### ■ Exhibit C: Notes on a Specific Task

Ms. Campbell points out that there are six students with individualized education plans in that class. She also explains how she alters the activities between her honors and college prep Level 2 classes: "Usually, for the honors I give them a verb bank and they have to put the correct verb in the sentence and then conjugate it. But for the other levels, I just give them the verb that they have to conjugate in the sentence. These kids do better with additional drills." She continues, "You're going to have to teach classes like that, but then you get your honors, too."

## I. PRE-CASE DISCUSSION PROBLEMS SETS

Complete the chart after reading the case.

| | |
|---|---|
| Facts | |
| Opinions | |
| Assumptions | |
| Theories referred or connected to (if any) | |
| Ambiguous language | |
| Criteria you used in analyzing the case (e.g., emotional vs. rational) | |
| Emerging options | |

Write a pre-case discussion decision paper. Include these points:

    a. options for case resolution

    b. criteria (a rational decision should always be made with a set of criteria)

    c. analysis of options

    d. recommendation (of the best choice among the options)

    e. action plan

## II. CASE DISCUSSION QUESTIONS

### Big-Picture Analysis

Describe the context of the case.

- institutional setting
- student demographics
- school structure and schedule

### Stakeholders

In small groups, assume the role of one of the case stakeholders. Write a statement/ dialogue expressing this person's or group's hypothetical feelings and perspectives. Be prepared to act out your roles to the large group.

- Ms. Campbell
- students in College Preparatory Class
- students in Honors Class
- Ms. Young

### Surface Issues

What are the surface issues in this case? What is happening here from an untrained perspective? What underlying assumptions or beliefs feed into this perspective?

### Deep Issues

Discuss the real issues in the case. Try to categorize them in terms of language teaching curriculum and instruction.

### Evidence-Based Solutions

In groups, develop evidence-based solutions for each deep issue listed. Whenever possible, refer to a theory or principle of language learning and teaching to support your proposed solutions.

### Teacher Thinking

In what ways does this case influence and/or reinforce your beliefs and dispositions as a teacher? Consult the Further Resources section to help with theoretically informed solutions.

## III. POST-CASE PROBLEM SETS

### Post-Case Analysis

A. Categorize what you learned as:
- teacher knowledge and praxis (e.g., content knowledge, curricular knowledge, pedagogical content knowledge and application)
- teacher thinking (e.g., beliefs, problem-solving strategies, prioritizing objectives, values, professional ethics, attitudes)

B. List:
- learning objectives that you discovered in the case
- potential learning outcomes
- implications for your pedagogical practices

C. The post-case problem sets introduce reactions from various perspectives. These quotes are from others who have read the cases for educational and pedagogical purposes. Read all of the quotes and then choose two about which to write a short response (put the quotes at the top of each response). Use these questions as a guide:
- What is the message the speaker is trying to convey? If possible, also explain why you chose the quote.
- What examples can you think of that connect to the themes presented?
- Can you relate the quote to a class discussion or to something you have read or experienced?

Quotes

1. "Students who do not have college as a goal should not be forced to take foreign language classes. The students, parents, and administrators never really view those courses as core for the 'ironically labeled' college preparatory classes."

2. "The teacher has no clear objectives and the lesson is not relevant or meaningful."

3. "The teacher is doing the best she can with a tough situation. The fact is some classes are just more difficult than others. It sounds bad but it is just reality."

4. "The teacher needs to have a warm-up activity to start the class and stimulate learner interest. Collecting homework is an ineffective way to increase learner motivation."

5. "The train station vocabulary could have been taught in varied ways."

D. Write a reflection describing a take-away from the case in terms of praxis. Make sure to develop an action plan to resolve the case. Consider these questions as guidelines:

- In what ways did the case discussion influence your thinking about the case?
- Did you change your original decision or did the discussion reaffirm your position?
- What points had you not considered prior to the case discussion?
- How might the information you gained from this case be applicable to your current instructional setting and/or future instructional settings?
- What did you learn?
- What are you inspired to learn more about?
- How did the themes discussed in class apply to your experience?

E. Discuss what theoretical basis there is for:

- the stakeholders' behavior in the case.
- the solutions you proposed.

## Further Reading and Resources

ACTFL. (1999). National Standards for Foreign Language Learning. Washington, DC: ACTFL.

Cole, D., Hood, P., & Marsh, D. (2010). *Content and language integrated learning.* Cambridge, England: Cambridge University Press.

Ellis, R. (2003). *Task-based language learning and teaching.* New York: Oxford University Press.

Kaufman, D., & Crandall, J. (Eds.) (2005). *Content-based instruction in primary and secondary school settings.* Alexandria, VA: TESOL.

Nunan, D. (1991). Communicative tasks and the language curriculum. *TESOL Quarterly, (25)*2, 279–295.

Nunan, D. (2005). *Practical English language teaching: Grammar.* New York: McGraw-Hill.

# ▪▪▪▪▪▪▪▪▪▪▪▪▪▪▪▪▪▪ CASE 4.2 ▪▪▪▪▪▪▪▪▪▪▪▪▪▪▪▪▪▪

# Charles Watson High

Charles Watson High School (CWHS) is the public high school serving a medium-sized city in the northeast part of the U.S. Students either come to CWHS from one of eleven public elementary (K–8) schools or from private schools and from other towns. CWHS was originally two separate schools: Marion High, founded in 1780, and the Watson Technical School, founded in 1888. It was not until 1983 that the two schools were merged into CWHS.

The high number of students taking Spanish prompted the department to create a standardized curriculum to ensure that all students (for example, in Spanish III) have been taught the same topics, regardless of who their teachers were the previous year. The standardized curriculum includes expectations on student outcomes, required projects, and standard tests, yet also has enough flexibility for the teachers to weave in their creative ideas.

The other world languages classes, however, have no standardized curriculum. Dr. Singer, the World Languages department head for the school system has declared, that "provided that the students continue to have a high achievement rate on the AP exam, I am satisfied that the teaching and learning in those classrooms meets objectives."

Ms. Cescut has been teaching French at CWHS for more than 22 years. Dr. Singer praises her for the quality of both her teaching and her native-like proficiency. In the spring, she taught three courses—French 2, French 4 Honors, and AP French. Each world language class is allotted 40 minutes during which to use the language lab; Ms. Cescut's French 2 class spends the majority of this language lab time working with a video series called *Reality France*.

*Reality France* is a French language video course in which a major portion of each episode features a scene between the recurring characters and focuses on a grammar and/or vocabulary theme. The main characters are Paulette (a French university student) and Alex (an American visiting Paris). For example, an episode about cars and transportation follows Paulette as she tries to visit a friend in the countryside. She rents a car and experiences a host of problems: The brakes fail, she runs out of gas, she gets a flat tire, the windshield wipers do not work, and, when she finally arrives at the friend's house, she has to turn around immediately, so as to be back before dark because the headlights do not work.

The scene lasts about 17 minutes and is fairly cohesive, although occasionally a mime cuts into a scene to act out some rather challenging verb phrases. At the end of 17 minutes, the professor in the video walks the viewers through the scene again, slowly and with much repeating and restating, going over vocabulary, with the occasional subtitle on screen. Many of the episodes end with segments of (unscripted) interviews with "real" French people about one of the cultural subjects tackled during the episode. In the episode on cars and transportation, for example, the survey questions include, "Is it difficult/dangerous to drive in Paris? Is it hard to get your driver's license in France?" The videos also often include one scene that has been edited so that the students can say the lines along with the characters. This part is usually about five lines of dialogue.

Ms. Cescut's students watch the video and are expected to take notes on what happened in the scene as well as vocabulary they pick up on. The students are told to list all the vocabulary that the teacher has written on the board, or as much as they can pick up from the screen, where the subtitles appear for approximately 12 seconds.

At the end of the 40-minute language lab time, the class returns to the classroom to discuss the episode. Using the accompanying teacher's guide, Ms. Cescut asks the students questions about what happened and about vocabulary, grammar, and idiomatic expressions that were used. The class reviews as much lexical material as possible until the period ends. This is conducted via a very simple interaction where Ms. Cescut asks questions in French, such as "*Comment dit-on* steering wheel?"

| | |
|---|---|
| Ms. Cescut: | "What happened when Paulette was driving down the country lane?" |
| Jane: | "She got a flat tire." |
| Ms. Cescut: | "Who helped her?" |
| Jane: | "A cyclist." |

Ms. Cescut usually waits for a student to raise his or her hand but she will occasionally call on somebody to answer. It sometimes seems that students have not heard the vocabulary enough to be certain of the pronunciation. and so make a best guess. For example, after viewing the episode on driving, the class lists the vocabulary they heard. When Ciara attempts to pronounce a vocabulary word, it sounds as though she says, "cray ver oon peuh noo." Ms. Cescut asks her to repeat it four or five times before she demands an English translation of what she said. It turns out Ciara meant "get a flat tire" (*crever un pneu*). Ms. Cescut then provides the correct pronunciation for students and spells it out on the board.

Of the ten students in the class, three or four participate in this type of exchange regularly. Ms. Cescut is unsure whether the other students do not participate because they did not understand the language in the video, they were not paying attention during the viewing, they did not take notes, they think school is uncool, or because they do not like the class.

When the bell sounds, the students rush out the door.

## ■ Exhibit A: School Profile

Approximately 1,700 students are enrolled at CWHS. The purpose of the learning communities (LCs) is to "foster excellence, learning and achievement for all students," according to the CWHS website, which adds, "Students take their core freshman and sophomore year classes within their LC and stay with this cohort for guidance counseling for all four years." CWHS has a student to teacher ratio of 16:1, but actual class sizes vary greatly. Some class sizes are as big as 35 students. CWHS offers honors courses in the core subjects of English, history, mathematics, science, and world languages, as well as AP courses in these subjects to students in the eleventh and twelfth grades. CWHS is on a block schedule with each core subject meeting for 80 minutes, five times a week, for one semester. There are a total of four periods in the school day. At the beginning of each semester, students begin new courses.

## ■ Exhibit B: World Languages Program Structure

The World Languages Department at CWHS offers instruction in five languages: Spanish, French, Italian, Latin, and Portuguese. The CWHS website explains the school's view of language study: "One of the most critical 21$^{st}$ century academic studies in the roster of CWHS courses is world language. The study of another language gives an inside perspective of another culture, way of thinking, set of values, beliefs and lifestyles; it is the most natural tool for gaining a multicultural outlook; it advances English vocabulary and knowledge of language structure and usage. It is pivotal for college and career readiness." Clearly, language study is highly valued.

Approximately 78 percent of students at CWHS take Spanish. Of the remaining 22 percent, the majority takes French, and the other three languages, Italian, Latin, and Portuguese, have a fairly even representative distribution. So, while the average Spanish class consists of 25 to 30 students, the average French class has 9 to 15.

## I. Pre-Case Discussion Problems Sets

Complete the chart after reading the case.

| | |
|---|---|
| Facts | |
| Opinions | |
| Assumptions | |
| Theories referred or connected to (if any) | |
| Ambiguous language | |
| Criteria you used in analyzing the case (e.g., emotional vs. rational) | |
| Emerging options | |

Write a pre-case discussion decision paper. Include these points:

a. options for case resolution

b. criteria (a rational decision should always be made with a set of criteria)

c. analysis of options

d. recommendation (of the best choice among the options)

e. action plan

## II. CASE DISCUSSION QUESTIONS

### *Big-Picture Analysis*

Describe the context of the case.

- What can you tell about the student population and how might that impact learning?
- What do we know about the school structure, specifically, learning communities?
- What resources are available for FL teachers?
- What do we know about the French curriculum? Is this an evidence-based curricular design?

### *Stakeholders*

In small groups, assume the role of one of the case stakeholders. Write a statement/dialogue expressing this person's or group's hypothetical feelings and perspectives. Be prepared to act out your roles to the large group.

- Ms. Cescut
- Jane
- Ciara
- a colleague observing the class

### *Surface Issues*

What are the surface issues in this case? What is happening here from an untrained perspective? What underlying assumptions or beliefs feed into this perspective?

### *Deep Issues*

Discuss the real issues in the case. Try to categorize them in terms of language teaching curriculum and instruction.

### *Evidence-Based Solutions*

In groups, develop evidence-based solutions for each deep issue listed. Whenever possible, refer to a theory or principle of language learning and teaching to support your proposed solutions.

## III. Post-Case Problem Sets

### *Post-Case Analysis*

A. Categorize what you learned as:
- teacher knowledge and praxis (e.g., content knowledge, curricular knowledge, pedagogical content knowledge and application)
- teacher thinking (e.g., beliefs, problem-solving strategies, prioritizing objectives, values, professional ethics, attitudes)

B. List:
- learning objectives that you discovered in the case
- potential learning outcomes
- implications for your pedagogical practices

C. The post-case problem sets introduce reactions from various perspectives. These quotes are from others who have read the cases for educational and pedagogical purposes. Read all of the quotes and then choose two about which to write a short response (put the quotes at the top of each response).  Use these questions as a guide:
- What is the message the speaker is trying to convey? If possible, also explain why you chose the quote.
- What examples can you think of that connect to the themes presented?
- Can you relate the quote to a class discussion or to something you have read or experienced?

Quotes

1. "Solely relying on technology to do the work of teaching students is not just or fair. A video cannot substitute for a teacher. A video cannot talk back to students and cannot answer questions or ask questions. Technology in general should be used in the classroom to either introduce, review, or reinforce a topic or lesson. One should not rely on technology to do all the teaching. The 17-minute video segments are way too long. The teacher needs to spend more time in the classroom and less time having her students watching a video."

2. "Based on the snapshot from the case, I believe the teacher could alter her approach to the material. She has been doing the same thing day in and day out, and it has not been working. She could develop pre- and post-language lab work that would put the lab work in context and better prepare students for what the video is going to cover. She could also revise the work she has the students doing during the video to allow them to be more successful."

3. "Using technology for the sake of technology is a problem that can easily occur in my classroom. I confess that I have never taken my students to the language lab, but I do a lot of supplementary work in the classroom. I do a lot of work with my students involving current music and pop culture. It is hard to introduce these and keep them in context with the textbook or whatever novel we are reading, but it is important to find some kind of connection so that my students can make deeper connections, and so that they won't spend time puzzling over questions like 'Why are we doing this?' and 'What's the point?'"

D. Write a reflection describing a take-away from the case in terms of praxis. Make sure to develop an action plan to resolve the case. Consider these questions as guidelines:

- In what ways did the case discussion influence your thinking about the case?
- Did you change your original decision or did the discussion reaffirm your position?
- What points had you not considered prior to the case discussion?

- How might the information you gained from this case be applicable to your current instructional setting and/or future instructional settings?
- What did you learn?
- What are you inspired to learn more about?
- How did the themes discussed in class apply to your experience?

E. Discuss what theoretical basis there is for:

- the stakeholders' behavior in the case.
- the solutions you proposed.

## Further Reading and Resources

Baird, K., & Redmond, M. (Eds.). (2004). *The use of authentic materials in the K–12 French program*. Winston-Salem, NC: Wake Forest University Department of Education.

Field, J. (2008). *Listening in the language classroom*. Cambridge, England: Cambridge University Press. http://dx.doi.org/10.1017/cbo9780511575945

Nunan, D., & Miller, L. (Eds.). (1995). *New ways in teaching listening*. Alexandria, VA: TESOL.

Omaggio-Hadley, A. (2001). *Teaching language in context* (3rd ed.). Boston: Heinle & Heinle.

Peacock, M. (1997). The effect of authentic materials on the motivation of EFL learners. *ELT Journal, 51*(2), 144–156. http://dx.doi.org/10.1093/elt/51.2.144

Rubin, J. (1995). The contribution of video to the development of competence in listening. In D.J. Mendelsohn & J. Rubin (Eds.), *A guide for the teaching of second language listening* (pp. 151–165). San Diego, CA: Dominie Press.

Wiggins, G. (1994). Toward more authentic assessment of language performance. In C. R. Hancock (Ed.), *Teaching, testing, and assessment: Making the connection* (pp. 69–85). Lincolnwood, IL: National Textbook Company.

Zyzik, E., & Polio, C. (2017). *Authentic materials myths: Applying second language research to classroom teaching*. Ann Arbor: University of Michigan Press.

▪▪▪▪▪▪▪▪▪▪▪▪▪▪▪▪▪ CASE 4.3 ▪▪▪▪▪▪▪▪▪▪▪▪▪▪▪▪▪

# Descartes Immersion School

Descartes is a public high school in an affluent, predominantly white suburb of a major U.S. city. Mr. Green teaches here; he had a privileged upbringing. He was born and raised in an affluent community with parents who put him in the best private schools in the region. He went on to attend a small, elite, liberal arts college. However, his career path did not take the direction he expected. He went to college with the full intention of becoming a Latin teacher, and while he accomplished this goal, he also picked up French along the way. He ended his academic career with a minor in French and had the pleasure of living in France for a few years after graduating from college. Hoping to be a highly sought-after teaching candidate at a top-notch private or high-performing public high school, he decided to take his certification exam not only for Latin but for French as well. He passed and was licensed to teach both languages.

Mr. Green's first few years at Descartes Immersion School were spent teaching Latin. As the popularity of the course decreased, however, Mr. Green started teaching French to complete his schedule. Over the years, Mr. Green found himself teaching more and more French classes and fewer and fewer Latin classes. At the beginning of the current school year, for the first time ever, Mr. Green found himself teaching only French classes, something he thought would never happen.

The school system Mr. Green settled in was a unique one. It was the only school in the area that featured a French immersion program. A little concerned about teaching a population of learners he had no experience with, he sought advice from colleagues during lunch time one day.

"So, my French classes are full of Haitian immigrant students this year. Does anyone else have such a class makeup?" he inquired. Ms. Bush, a fellow science teacher at the school, exclaimed, "They are all French-speaking Haitian heritage learners, so your class should be a breeze for them."

As Mr. Green started the school year, he noticed some interesting trends in his classes. Those that were comprised of students in the immersion program were more than 95 percent white, and the majority of them were from affluent families. In these classes, there was nearly gender balance with a slightly higher number of females. The classes consisting of higher-level students and of students who had dropped out of the immersion program but wanted to continue taking French were of a more equal mix in terms of race, with more males than females. His biggest concern, however, was his fourth year class, consisting of students who had never been a part of the immersion program and for whom, in subsequent years, foreign languages would no longer be a requirement but an elective.

This particular class was dominated by Haitian heritage learners. In the class of sixteen students, only two were of the non-Caribbean minority. There were only three boys in the entire class. All of the students spoke fluent English, but Haitian Creole was the predominant language spoken in their households. Many of the girls were taking Creole classes outside of school in order to be more connected to their heritage.

As a whole, the class consisted of good students, but they did not seem eagerly engaged or interested in the content. Given the fact that they were heritage language learners, he could not understand their lack of enthusiasm. It felt as though they were completely disconnected from the content and just going through the motions of the course without active participation.

For each of his thematic units, Mr. Green would include authentic resources from France, and he was known in the school for designing student-centered classes. This month's unit was on the theme of "Sensationalism in the French Media." In addition to the textbook, a typical CLT text, he provided students with these French-based news sources:

- http://www.parismatch.com/
- http://fr.yahoo.com/
- http://www.tv5.org/TV5Site/7-jours/
- http://www.france24.com/fr/
- http://www.lemonde.fr/

In an attempt to understand why this particular group of students was "low energy," he shared both the general unit outline and language outcomes and an excerpt from his most recent lesson plan with a colleague during lunch (see Exhibit B). He explained to her that the students completed the assignments with lots of prodding but they really lacked luster when it came to presentations of their personal analysis and opinions. Ms. Bush told Mr. Green, "This unit plan is stellar! Sometimes getting enthusiastic learners is the luck of the draw. You never know what you are going to get and some years are better than others. Just keep at it," she said. "Hopefully, they will draw some inspiration from your class."

During the next class meeting with this group, Mr. Green asked his students to do these tasks:

1. Present a news story to the class, using media sources and Parts A, B, C, D, and E of the chart that was completed in Interpretive Activity # 3.
2. As an optional follow-up presentational activity, find an authentic and objective news story and then role-play (oral or written) as a journalist for a "sensationalist" news agency. The job is to sensationalize the news story to appeal to a certain demographic group.

No one volunteered to present. After losing his patience, Mr. Green yelled at the students: "I don't know why no one is volunteering. You all have French-speaking backgrounds. This class should help you feel more connected to your language culture and help you to develop a sense of pride." Then, one student remarked under his breath to another in Creole, *"Sa a se pa ki gen rapò ak kilti nou an!"* ("This news is not related to our culture!")

Guetchina, one of higher-performing Haitian girls, stayed after class and tried to diplomatically explain to the teacher that the issue is that they are not accustomed to group work and group presentations; she thinks the class is better when the teacher is at the front of the room leading the way. She tried to tell Mr. Green about some differences between Haitian and French language and culture, but the bell rang and she had to run to her next class.

When it came to grammar, reading, and writing tasks from the textbook, students always moved along Mr. Green's schedule at a regular pace and never seemed to struggle too much with the content. The problem with the fourth level class was their lack of overall engagement and reluctance and often refusal to actually speak French in the classroom.

Mr. Green tried as hard as he could to immerse his students in the language. He taught about 80 percent of the class in French, reverting to English only when the students had problems understanding grammar concepts. When prodded, his students could supply the correct answers in French, but they refused to use the target language to ask questions about the work or for permission (to go to their locker or the restroom). Mr. Green often pushed and pushed to get his students to speak French, but sometimes for the sake of time—and his sanity—he had to allow them to use English. He was actually rather surprised that, with so many of his students being able to speak French, they were all so reluctant.

Mr. Green did not know what to do with his students. They were all very bright and had a firm grasp of the language, but for some reason refused to speak. He was hesitant to be too hard on them because, for many, this year of French would determine whether or not they would continue taking the language as an elective. He wanted his students to enjoy themselves and keep their interest in the language, but at the same time he knew he was failing at improving their oral skills. He often tried to infuse culture into the classroom, but as evidenced with the French news activity, this strategy did not seem to lead to increased learner motivation. Placing a higher emphasis on the oral aspects of his curriculum was an option, but there was hardly enough time to do everything he needed to in the first place. He had to find a way to motivate his students to speak in French more.

## ■ Exhibit A: School Profile

Students in the immersion program of this public high school in an affluent suburb start taking French in the first grade and many of them continue through high school. The school borders a much less affluent town, and the area of the city around this border is of a much lower socio-economic class than the majority of the school system. As a result, there are a lot of minority students attending the city's only high school. The majority of these students are first- or second-generation Haitian immigrants.

## ■ Exhibit B: Mr. Green's Lesson Plan

**Unit Theme:** Communications and Media

**Unit Topic(s):** Sensationalism in the Media

**Essential Question(s):** What does sensationalism in the media look like? Why does it exist?

**Communicative Context:** Present, discuss, and debate the effects of and reasons for sensationalism in the media.

## UNIT LEARNING OUTCOMES
**Interpretive:**

- I can understand the main idea of texts related to everyday life and personal interests or studies.
- I can understand questions regarding something I have read.

**Interpersonal:**

Lesson:
1. Each student will be asked to find two media resources addressing the same news story. One source should be a "sensationalized" version of the news story; the other source should be an "objective" version of the same news story. Media resources do not have to be the same medium (e.g., one could be a video; one could be a written article).

2. Student will make a Venn diagram or other graphic outlining differences and similarities in the stories.

3. Student will complete a chart, with the following information:
   a. origin of the resource
   b. justification/details supporting an opinion of whether it is sensationalized or objective
   c. critique of the information (biased, fair, subjective, persuasive, politically motivated, ulterior motive)
   d. whether the information should be presented in a different way, and how
   e. effect of the report on the student personally, or how it might affect various demographic groups of readers
   f. student's personal analysis, critique or opinion of each media resource (e.g., the reasons for and the effects of the various types of reporting presented)

## ▌ Exhibit C: Cross-Cultural Information

In Haiti, the majority of education is teacher-centered. Students are rarely expected to speak up and share their thoughts, ideas, or opinions.

## I. Pre-Case Discussion Problems Sets

Complete the chart after reading the case.

| | |
|---|---|
| Facts | |
| Opinions | |
| Assumptions | |
| Theories referred or connected to (if any) | |
| Ambiguous language | |
| Criteria you used in analyzing the case (e.g., emotional vs. rational) | |
| Emerging options | |

Write a pre-case discussion decision paper. Include these points:

a. options for case resolution

b. criteria (a rational decision should always be made with a set of criteria)

c. analysis of options

d. recommendation (of the best choice among the options)

e. action plan

## II. CASE DISCUSSION QUESTIONS

### Big-Picture Analysis

Describe the context of the case.

- institutional setting
- student demographics
- physical resources
- curricular mandate

### Stakeholders

In small groups, assume the role of one of the case stakeholders. Write a statement/dialogue expressing this person's or group's hypothetical feelings and perspectives. Be prepared to act out your roles to the large group.

- Mr. Green
- Guetchina
- student who said, "This is not our culture."
- the rest of the students in the class
- Ms. Bush

### Surface Issues

What are the surface issues in this case? What is happening here from an untrained perspective? What underlying assumptions or beliefs feed into this perspective?

### Deep Issues

Discuss the real issues in the case. Try to categorize them in terms of language teaching curriculum and instruction.

### *Evidence-Based Solutions*

In groups, develop evidence-based solutions for each deep issue listed. Whenever possible, refer to a theory or principle of language learning and teaching to support your proposed solutions.

### *Teacher Thinking*

In what ways does this case influence and/or reinforce your beliefs and dispositions as a teacher? Consult the Further Resources section to help with theoretically informed solutions.

## III. POST-CASE PROBLEM SETS

### *Post-Case Analysis*

A. Categorize what you learned as:
- teacher knowledge and praxis (e.g., content knowledge, curricular knowledge, pedagogical content knowledge and application)
- teacher thinking (e.g., beliefs, problem-solving strategies, prioritizing objectives, values, professional ethics, attitudes)

B. List:
- learning objectives that you discovered in the case
- potential learning outcomes
- implications for your pedagogical practices

C. The post-case problem sets introduce reactions from various perspectives. These quotes are from others who have read the cases for educational and pedagogical purposes. Read all of the quotes and then choose two about which to write a short response (put the quotes at the top of each response). Use these questions as a guide:
- What is the message the speaker is trying to convey? If possible, also explain why you chose the quote.
- What examples can you think of that connect to the themes presented?
- Can you relate the quote to a class discussion or to something you have read or experienced?

Quotes

1. "I always thought that French and Haitian Creole were basically the same. Could a person speaking French and a person speaking Creole communicate?"

2. "Most of the students in Mr. Green's classroom speak Haitian Creole, but he disregarded a cultural aspect of Haitian Creole and French and the connections between these two languages."

3. "The class discussion also reminded me of the importance of using the 5 Cs (ACTFL) in language teaching. The situation for Mr. Green would be greatly improved by the incorporation of these five things. These standards exist to help to help students develop all aspects of language."

4. "The teacher just needs to be stricter with the students and tell them directly that their success or failure of the class is dependent on their oral participation."

5. "The students in any French class, especially this one, would truly benefit from having an ample supply of authentic material from across regions in France and from across a range of Francophone or French post-colonial countries. This authentic material could be in the form of a menu from a French vs. Haitian restaurant, a CD from a famous singers in France, or a cheese tasting from the different regions of France. French culture is so rich and exciting that I am sure it would not be too much trouble to find some enlightening material. In this case, they could look at news broadcasts from Haiti and France. Why not?"

D. Write a reflection describing a take-away from the case in terms of praxis. Make sure to develop an action plan to resolve the case. Consider these questions as guidelines:

- In what ways did the case discussion influence your thinking about the case?

- Did you change your original decision or did the discussion reaffirm your position?

- What points had you not considered prior to the case discussion?
- How might the information you gained from this case be applicable to your current instructional setting and/or future instructional settings?
- What did you learn?
- What are you inspired to learn more about?
- How did the themes discussed in class apply to your experience?

E. Discuss what theoretical basis there is for:

- the stakeholders' behavior in the case.
- the solutions you proposed.

## Further Reading and Resources

Ballenger, C. (1999) *Teaching other people's children: Literacy and learning in a bilingual classroom.* New York: Teachers College Press.

Byram, M., & Morgan, C. (1994). *Teaching and learning language and culture.* Clevedon, England: Multilingual Matters.

Byram, M., Nichols, A., & Stevens, D. (Eds.). (2001). *Developing intercultural competence in practice.* Clevedon, England: Multilingual Matters.

Dörnyei, Z., & Ushioda, E. (2013). *Teaching and researching: Motivation* (2nd ed.). New York: Routledge.

Gardner, R. C. (2011). The socio-educational model of second language acquisition. *Canadian Issues,* 24–27.

Kramsch, C. (1993). *Context and culture in language teaching.* Oxford, England: Oxford University Press.

Theisen, T. (2002). Differentiated instruction in the foreign language classroom: Meeting the diverse needs of all learners. *LOTE CED Communiqué, Issue 6.* Austin, TX: LOTE Center for Educator Development.

# Chapter 5

# Cases in Post-Secondary English for Academic Purposes

The cases in this chapter deal with the complexity of the EAP classroom at the post-secondary level. Case 5.1, *Morrell Community College*, highlights the importance of a pedagogical rationale blending content and language objectives to develop student competences in academic culture and language. Case 5.2, *Greenview University*, tackles a problem that plagues the writing classroom and college administrators alike, and focuses on the moves involved in the writing process which—if modeled appropriately—will bridge cultural differences and cultivate academic integrity. The final case (5.3), *Lakeborough College*, presents the risks of confusing EAP and general language teaching and emphasizes the importance of developing cultural awareness along with academic skills.

■■■■■■■■■■■■■■■■■ CASE 5.1 ■■■■■■■■■■■■■■■■■

# Morrell Community College

The first-year composition class meets in a basement room in a typical urban setting. Even though students come from a variety of privileged departments (sciences, engineering, business) with state-of-the-art facilities, the students in this foundational academic skills class are assigned to meet in a semi-dark, dingy environment. The 15 or so students huddle in one corner of the large room; most are staring at their phones and some are whispering. Dr. Spurns walks into the room with a booming greeting.

"What are we doing today?" he asks.

Then, "What is the homework? Who's presenting?"

The quick questions go unanswered, but there are some murmurs in the corner. Dr. Spurns scribbles a few bullets on the board:

- Discussion
- Quiz
- Group work
- Presentation
- GRAMMAR

"You know the routine: Get into your groups, 1, 2, 3!"

This command results in some shuffling, tables being pushed around, pencils dropping, and laptops opening.

Dr. Spurns has already listed several points on the board:

1. Native Americans
2. Montana
3. World War II
4. Native American Reservations

"Group 1, take Native Americans. Group 2, Montana. Group 3, World War II. All groups also take the fourth one, Native American reservations. Tell us what you know about that. Five minutes!"

The students are finally in groups. Some of the groups are all male, while others all female; a few are mixed gender. Judging by appearance, different ethnicities are represented in most groups, but there are no detectable patterns in the class that is two-thirds Asian and one-third Caucasian. Whispered words in some groups suggest a predominance of Chinese. Many of the students look puzzled. A tentatively raised hand gets Dr. Spurns' attention:

"Professor, what kind of information do you want from us?"

"Anything you know about your topic!" he responds.

"Do you mean history, geography, or just vocabulary?"

"Didn't you read the first chapter of the book?" asks Dr. Spurns.

Another tentative hand goes up. "But, you told us to take notes."

"Yes, on everything! I'll walk around and check your reading logs," Dr. Spurns replies.

Dr. Spurns then starts pacing and peeking over the students' shoulders. In some groups, papers rustle in the otherwise silent room. One phone rings several times, and its jazzy tone is met with chuckles. A boy with the adopted American name of Brad says to the girl next to him: "Why don't you take notes for our group?"

"It's always me," she complains. Then she opens her notebook with pen in hand.

Dr. Spurns then says, "Over! Let's hear what you have. Any volunteers?"

The silence is complete.

"Amanda?"

Amanda does not look up. Most of the students do not look up.

Brad speaks up: "The Native Americans were the first on this continent. The English who came, you know the emigrants, killed a lot of them."

"The settlers, you mean? Where did the Native Americans live mostly?" Dr. Spurns asks.

Slowly, the class responds with a word here or there. Dr. Spurns writes some of what he hears on the board, but not all of it. Comments cover points 1, 2, 3, but not 4. The students have significantly more to say about World War II, in impressive detail, in fact.

Dr. Spurns moves on briskly: "Two more minutes and then we do the quiz."

There is more shuffling of papers and some worried faces while the quiz is distributed. The quiz consists of three sections: vocabulary (*List the words in Chapter 1 you found useful and explain why*); grammar (*Identify and correct the errors in the five sentences*); multiple choice (*Answer the questions to provide factual information contained in Chapters 1 and 2*). The time allocated is 20 minutes.

The students work diligently. Then Dr. Spurns springs into action:

"Done! On to the presentation!"

A team of three students reports what it found about the background of the story in the novel: the geography and demographics of the small town, the major and minor characters, and interesting vocabulary items. They take turns reading from their notes, but occasionally trip over each other's cues, as some are clearly more fluent than others. The class is mostly attentive: Some students take notes, but others look only at their phones. The presentation wraps up with muted applause.

"Let's do some grammar now," Dr. Spurns announces, and the remaining ten minutes of the class are spent on exercises that illustrate challenges with prepositions and articles.

"You know the routine for next class! Have a good day!"

The students file out in their preferred clusters.

## ■ Exhibit A: Institutional Context

This EAP course is at the entry level in a community college composition program. The curricular emphasis is on academic acculturation with a goal of facilitating the language skills of L2 students who are typically in the first semester of first year. In such programs, the makeup of the class may vary from quite diverse to just a few groups as in this situation. The goals of the course are rigorously academic, including advanced language proficiency and key academic competences. Here is a representative sampling:

- Use effective strategies for critically reading complex texts.
- Identify and practice various writing styles and formats.
- Express ideas using a controlled range of structures.
- Acquire knowledge of advanced grammar and basic metalanguage.
- Fluently perform classroom language functions.
- Understand the culture of the academic classroom.

Assigned readings provide models for analysis and discussion that help students recognize and emulate the processes used in academic texts. A successful completion of the course expects L2 students to achieve a balance of language skills that would allow them to perform competently—and on a par with native peers—the academic tasks relevant to their field of study. The instructors in the program have credentials in TESOL and pedagogical experience in L2 writing.

## ▮ Exhibit B: Presentation Outline

*Section I: Analysis of Theme*

Choose three eloquent passages. Each passage should represent a different theme that you have identified within the text.

*Section II: Analysis of Rhetorical Technique*

Choose three short passages that illustrate unique rhetorical points. Choose from:

- repetition
- metaphor
- simile
- symbolism
- definition
- tense shift
- tone shift
- irony
- satire
- dialect or non-standard usage

*Section III: Vocabulary*

Note three new vocabulary items key to understanding the text. Write out the entire sentence from the text and underline the unfamiliar word/expression.

*Section IV: Discussion Questions*

Formulate three insightful discussion questions, at least one of which connects to other readings from our textbook. Aim for a variety of questions. Discussion leaders should involve ALL students in the discussion. This forum is meant to foster a lively intellectual exchange of ideas.

*Section V: Grammar Focus Point*

Discover an interesting grammatical feature of the text (e.g., sentence structure, word order, punctuation). Research that feature and present a brief summary of your findings in class.

# I. PRE-CASE DISCUSSION PROBLEMS SETS

Complete the chart after reading the case.

| Facts | |
|---|---|
| Opinions | |
| Assumptions | |
| Theories referred or connected to (if any) | |
| Ambiguous language | |
| Criteria you used in analyzing the case (e.g., emotional vs. rational) | |
| Emerging options | |

Write a pre-case discussion decision paper. Include these points:

a. options for case resolution

b. criteria (a rational decision should always be made with a set of criteria)

c. analysis of options

d. recommendation (of the best choice among the options)

e. action plan

## II. CASE DISCUSSION QUESTIONS

### Big-Picture Analysis

Describe the context of the case.

- institutional setting
- student demographics
- physical resources
- curricular mandate

### Stakeholders

In small groups, assume the role of one of the case stakeholders. Write a statement/ dialogue expressing this person's or group's hypothetical feelings and perspectives. Be prepared to act out your roles to the large group.

- Dr. Spurns
- Brad
- Amanda
- the rest of the students in the class
- a program administrator observing the class

### Surface Issues

What are the surface issues in this case? What is happening here from an untrained perspective? What underlying assumptions or beliefs feed into this perspective?

### Deep Issues

Discuss the real issues in the case. Try to categorize them in terms of language teaching curriculum and instruction.

### *Evidence-Based Solutions*

In groups, develop evidence-based solutions for each deep issue listed. Whenever possible, refer to a theory or principle of language learning and teaching to support your proposed solutions.

### *Teacher Thinking*

In what ways does this case influence and/or reinforce your beliefs and dispositions as a teacher? Consult the Further Resources section to help with theoretically informed solutions.

## III. POST-CASE PROBLEM SETS

### *Post-Case Analysis*

A. Categorize what you learned as:
- teacher knowledge and praxis (e.g., content knowledge, curricular knowledge, pedagogical content knowledge and application)
- teacher thinking (e.g., beliefs, problem-solving strategies, prioritizing objectives, values, professional ethics, attitudes)

B. List:
- learning objectives that you discovered in the case
- potential learning outcomes
- implications for your pedagogical practices

C. The post-case problem sets introduce reactions from various perspectives. These quotes are from others who have read the cases for educational and pedagogical purposes. Read all of the quotes and then choose two about which to write a short response (put the quotes at the top of each response). Use these questions as a guide:
- What is the message the speaker is trying to convey? If possible, also explain why you chose the quote.
- What examples can you think of that connect to the themes presented?
- Can you relate the quote to a class discussion or to something you have read or experienced?

## Quotes

1. "The instructor seemed to want to pack a lot into the class in the form of drills. He kept referring to a routine, but I was wondering what the established sequence format was. Also, what exactly preceded that session? What were the students assigned to read? What other preparation did they have to do for the class?"

2. "My recommendation for this teacher is to mitigate his style. He is abrupt, impatient, and creates a boot camp atmosphere in the class. He should explore the background of his students and harness their knowledge about the topic (not quite sure what that is, though). He is inconsistent: he acts very strict about time-keeping but ignores other distractors in the class (L1, phones). I'd be curious about his course evaluations—do the students like him or fear him?"

3. "I am puzzled by the designation of the class as composition and writing-intensive. There was little writing involved in any of the activities except for the quiz. If I were a student, I would probably be OK with the minimal writing (as this is usually the hardest academic challenge), but I would also wonder what I would be graded on—the quiz? participation? The assessment criteria are fuzzy, and the instructor's feedback is minimal. There are no scaffolding materials of any kind to help the students deal with the new content (in fact not defined at all) and practice the relevant language skills."

4. "This being an EAP-oriented class, I would suggest that the agenda reflect that. As it is, discussion figures there, but there is very little of it during the session. Also, grammar is listed separately, but it is covered in a generic way, with exercises on across-levels problems such as articles and prepositions (which are, in fact, largely lexical issues). The instructor seems experienced and is probably able to get a lot of good work form the students, but he should plan the class much more carefully in terms of prepping the sequence of activities, providing opportunities to integrate all language skills in the service of academic communication, and allocating time for review and feedback."

D. Write a reflection describing a take-away from the case in terms of praxis. Make sure to develop an action plan to resolve the case. Consider these questions as guidelines:

- In what ways did the case discussion influence your thinking about the case?
- Did you change your original decision or did the discussion reaffirm your position?
- What points had you not considered prior to the case discussion?
- How might the information you gained from this case be applicable to your current instructional setting and/or future instructional settings?
- What did you learn?
- What are you inspired to learn more about?
- How did the themes discussed in class apply to your experience?

E. Discuss what theoretical basis there is for:

- the stakeholders' behavior in the case.
- the solutions you proposed.

## Further Reading and Resources

BALEAP. (2008). *BALEAP competency framework for teachers of English for academic purposes*. Retrieved from www.baleap.org

BALEAP. (2013). *BALEAP can-do framework for EAP syllabus design and assessment*. Retrieved from www.baleap.org.uk

Coxhead, A. (2000). A new academic word list. *TESOL Quarterly, 34*(2), 213–238.

Field, J. (Ed.) (2011). Special Issue: Listening in EAP. *Journal of English for Academic Purposes, 10*(2).

McCarter, S., and Jakes, P. (2009). *Uncovering EAP: How to teach academic writing and reading*. Oxford, England: Macmillan.

Nation, I.S.P. (2001). *Learning vocabulary in another language*. New York: Cambridge University Press.

Paterson, K., with Wedge, R. (2013). *Oxford grammar for EAP: English grammar and practice for academic purposes*. Oxford, England: Oxford University Press.

Reinhart, S.M. (2013). *Giving academic presentations* (2nd ed.). Ann Arbor: University of Michigan Press.

Tomlinson, B. (Ed.). (2011). *Materials development in language teaching* (2nd ed.). Cambridge, England: Cambridge University Press.

Purdue University Online Writing Lab (OWL). Retrieved from https://owl.english.purdue.edu/owl/resource/1002/01/

# ▪▪▪▪▪▪▪▪▪▪▪▪▪▪▪▪▪ CASE 5.2 ▪▪▪▪▪▪▪▪▪▪▪▪▪▪▪▪▪
# Greenview University

Hi Linda,

I am attaching the self-assessment, first draft, and final version of Paper 2 from a student who has pretty clearly plagiarized. He must have had someone write, or at least significantly revise, his paper to put it in perfect English—more likely had someone write it start to finish because the draft contains nothing of substance, just a bare outline (which was hastily submitted only when I prodded him about not having submitted a draft).

I've called him in to meet with me on Wednesday (though we'll have to see if he replies, since he ignored my last two messages, even though on the second one I cc'd his advisor). But I wanted to send these files to you in order to alert you of the situation—and also so that when I meet with him I can truthfully tell the student that I've already reported the situation to my department chair.

Thank you for your advice as always.

Becky

This message was the first one to welcome Linda, the director of ESL at Green-view, when she opened her Monday morning email. "Not another one," she thought, sighing. There had been a streak of plagiarism cases in the past couple of weeks—usual at this point in the semester when students were overwhelmed with mid-terms, projects, and paper deadlines before spring break. Some of the cases were clear cut: word-for-word passages dropped in the middle of drafts; a mosaic of paraphrased sentences and original writing; recurring gaps in citing. The explanations in the form of excuses were also predictable: "I did not realize this was plagiarism." "This seemed like the best way to say what I had in mind." "At this stage of drafting, I had forgotten where this piece came from… ."

The troubling recent development, however, was the increase in less "obvious" violations: excessive help from outside, either as collaboration, or plainly rewritten polished versions of the papers. Over the past three semesters, Becky had had an unfair share of those, and Linda felt bad for her. An energetic and innovative young teacher with a keen eye for detail, Becky was also an experienced writing center tutor, especially attuned to the needs of L2 writers. Caring but principled, Becky was quick to report a problem, following the rules of the university's *Aca-*

*demic Conduct Code.* Her first instinct was to give the student the benefit of the doubt and exploit the unfortunate situation as a teachable moment. She clarified the problem and gave the student an opportunity to revise, hoping to pre-empt future violations. So, the urgency of Becky's email signaled a bigger problem, one that might call for more drastic measures and involve the administration beyond the classroom.

Linda sighed again, reached for her cup of coffee, and opened the attachments.

On Thursday, Linda found this update in her mailbox:

> Hi Linda,
>
> I met with Eric (that's his American name) yesterday, and he insisted that the paper was his own work. I said that it did not sound like his own voice and asked if he could produce a draft that came between the brief outline he submitted and the polished final version. He said that he could, and in fact was able to immediately open up his laptop and email me a draft written "in his own voice."
>
> When I asked if anyone had helped him with his English, he said yes. He said he had gone back to his high school friend, a bilingual Chinese speaker with native-sounding English, with whom he had been working for years (including the entire freshman year at our university, he said...). This was under the guidance of his high school English teacher. He was very defensive and said it was highly beneficial to his learning English. I think I was able to communicate to him why it wasn't okay for two reasons. First, he had received too much help from this friend because the voice in the paper sounded nothing like his own, and second, he had completely bypassed our program's teaching and learning process—working with me, his professor, submitting a real draft to me, and revising based on my feedback. (And indeed, he had completely ignored the critique of his proposed argument that I made on the outline he sent me; I get the impression he never even opened the file with my feedback.)
>
> I believe Eric's story—that he did in fact write his own paper and that his mistake was receiving an inappropriate amount of help in revising it to sound like native English. The fact that he was able to produce his draft on the spot in my office confirms that he's likely telling the truth. When a student did something similar in my summer class, I seem to recall that I graded her draft and averaged that grade with the F on the plagiarized version. I am willing to allow Eric to remain in my class on these same terms (which he says he wants to do). He promises that he will not bypass the course's drafting process or receive an inappropriate amount of help again.

Does that sound reasonable to you? Once I hear back from you, I'll send Eric an email, cc'ing both the academic officer and his faculty advisor (although I have written to his faculty advisor already and not heard back, unfortunately), and telling him what the situation is and advising him to meet with the academic officer to discuss it.

Linda replied immediately, concurring with the plan to suggest a grading penalty and to allow the student to continue the course.

A few days later, Becky knocked on Linda's office door. She was clearly flustered. "Linda, I just met with Eric. He now refuses to accept the grading penalty. I don't know what else I can do. Could you talk with him, too?"

Eric stood somewhat timidly in Linda's office. After being invited to take a seat, he perched on the edge of a chair.

Linda began, "So, tell me what happened, Eric. Your instructor reports that you at first agreed but then declined the grading penalty."

Eric described how he had written the paper all by himself ("all the ideas were mine") and then had sent it to his friend to look over. He got the new version and incorporated the suggestions about "the language only."

He was a little startled when Linda asked whether he had read the *Academic Conduct Code* and whether he knew about "excessive collaboration."

"I know about plagiarism, but **I** wrote the paper," was his answer.

Linda explained why the paper had raised suspicion, both for the instructor and her: The draft was riddled with syntactic and lexical problems, whereas the final version was fluid. Also, the voice sounded native and sophisticated, not like anything that any L2 student at this level could have produced. She also outlined a fairly grim scenario of penalties and that there would need to be a hearing. Eric listened politely. Then he reiterated: "I'd like to explain to the committee that the paper is my own, my ideas. I'm not a cheater."

A half hour later, when he left, a weary Linda sat back at the computer to email Becky, feeling a sense of defeat creeping in.

The Academic Conduct Committee hearing was attended by the instructor, the department head, and the student, all of whom made brief statements from their perspectives. After a quick deliberation, the academic council found that Eric had committed plagiarism and recommended a sanction of "disciplinary probation," which banned him from extracurricular activities only.

Becky and Linda were left with a bitter sense of missing pedagogical closure.

## ■ Exhibit A: Note on Plagiarism and Multilingual Writers

Some cultures may consider the knowledge in classic texts common property and therefore not cite the original source in all cases. However, Western academic culture requires that any use of someone's original work must be identified and documented properly so that due credit is given for all intellectual property. Even though these rules may seem mere cultural conventions, they are non-negotiable and should be applied consistently to avoid plagiarism. Students should consult their instructors whenever in doubt about documentation and citation rules, as non-compliance has serious consequences in all academic settings.

## ■ Exhibit B: Eric's Self-Assessment at the Start of the Course

## Self-Assessment

As a international student, writing, listening, and speaking are the most difficult things to come over when I study abroad. Composition courses are the best class we can learn from in order to get better at listening, speaking, and especially writing. Through the pervious course, there is a process I called "finding my own voice." I have done my best to prove my grammar problems since writing the first and it seems that I did not do a bad job at express my own thoughts, however, just being able to express my own thoughts isn't enough. What I really learned is how to come up with good thought and use strong evidence to support it. So in the next writing course, I followed the advice of my teacher and classmates to reconstruct my way to approach the claims and finally learned how to create my argument and provide strong argument. In this class, I still have to be careful about my grammar and spelling. A lot more than that, I want to be a good writer, who is able to give some great thoughts and express his idea accurately.

## ■ Exhibit C: Excerpt from Eric's Draft

Being a good children's book is not only about sweet story and easy to read, but also about teaching children something important in real life. There are thousands of children's book in the world but not so many of them are well known by people and even less than that, the book can actually be called great children's book. And this book does both of it. Therefore, such book is absolutely good children's book in general. However, just being a good and well known children's book doesn't mean that it always good for any age children.

And author not only attracts children's interests in this book, but also using such lovely story teach children some basic history and life points. Without any doubt, this book just satisfies every requirement that being a good children's book.

Great children's book always can teach children something that are hard to be learned by themselves in real life. And especially, young children don't have much understanding about death. Author's purpose in this book is to help them to face the fact when it occurs. That is why it is a good children's book. It may benefit some older age children when they already have some value and thoughts, but not for young age children. Some negative emotion may gives people really bad mental shadow when they are young. For instant, scientific study believes that acrophobia often cause by shock of height when people at very young age. Therefore what children should read should be selected carefully. So as a good children's book not necessary good for any age children.

## ▌ Exhibit D: Excerpt (Conclusion) from the Final Paper

What makes a children's book great is when it can teach children about something that is hard to learn in real life. Young children especially have little ability to process difficult subjects like loss and death. The purpose in this book is to introduce these serious themes to help children build the tools that enable them to face this reality if and when it occurs in their own lives. Ultimately, however, I think this book is of more benefit to older children who can handle the fast transitions and difficult subject matter. Young children, on the other hand, may find the experience scarring, as sometimes negative emotions can cause severe trauma for the young. For instance, scientific study believes that acrophobia is often caused by a shock of height when people are at very young age. It's important, therefore, that parents carefully select what their children read. Even a great children's book like this is not necessarily good for all readers. The issues the author introduces here are crucial and ones that many children will face. By giving children the capacity to confront issues of death and loss, he empowers them to see death as more than just an ending, and love as an ever-renewing source of strength.

## ▋ Exhibit E: Samples of Becky's Emails during the Process

A. I believed Eric's Paper 1 to be plagiarized, and at first I thought it was probably written by another person, because he did not submit a substantive draft (just an outline) and because the voice sounded native and sophisticated, not like anything that any student in an ESL class at that level could have produced.

B. I'm writing to remind you that you need to come to my office in order to sign the paperwork agreeing to the grade penalty for excessive collaboration on Paper 1. Academic Advising also encourages you to follow up with them to discuss the implications of doing so. If you do not sign the paperwork agreeing to the penalty, the Advising office will set up an academic hearing.

C. After orally agreeing to the grading penalty with me, and then meeting with his advisor and Academic Advising, Eric never showed up to sign the paperwork as agreed. He would dodge out after class so I could never speak to him in person and didn't answer emails like this one. Eventually, as you know, we did have to set up a hearing and go through with it.

## ▋ Exhibit F: Becky's Statement for the Hearing

I believed Eric's Paper 1 to be plagiarized because he did not submit a substantive draft (just an outline) and because the voice in the final paper sounded native and sophisticated, not like anything that Eric had previously submitted either officially or unofficially, and in fact, not like anything a student taking an ESL writing class at that level could have produced. I showed the materials to my department head, and she agreed. When I asked him about it, Eric told me that the ideas in the paper were his own work. I said that it did not sound like his own voice, and asked if he could produce a draft written in his voice that came in between the brief outline he submitted and the polished final version. He was able to provide me with a draft written in his own voice upon request. However, he admitted that the native-sounding English and sophisticated language of the final version were the result of excessive collaboration with a high school friend. I believe that Eric received too much help from this friend because the voice in the paper sounds nothing like his own. Excessive collaboration of this nature is still plagiarism. I also pointed out to Eric that by doing this, he had completely bypassed the teaching and learning process — working with me, his professor, submitting a real draft to me, and revising it based on my feedback.

I believe that Eric did in fact write his own paper, and that his mistake was receiving an inappropriate amount of help in revising it to sound like native English. Still, the fact that he was able to produce his draft on the spot when I requested it in my office is evidence that he was making a good faith effort to do his own work. For these reasons, I am willing to mitigate the grading penalty by averaging the F grade on the plagiarized version with the grade that I would have given to the draft (the complete draft, not the outline). I am willing to allow Eric to remain in my class on these terms, on the condition that he promises that he will not bypass the course's drafting process or collaborate excessively again.

The statement I provided for the packet was what I originally submitted to Advising when I first confirmed the plagiarism of Paper 1. I want to add something more now that Eric has completed the rest of the semester. One of the things that I really wanted Eric to understand was that by bypassing the feedback and revision process that is so important to our writing courses, he not only ended up excessively collaborating, but he also cheated himself of learning the lessons about effective writing that I was trying to teach. He mistook grammatical correctness and sounding native for good writing. Eric promised me at the time that he would not bypass that process again, but he has only partially held up his end of the bargain. For Papers 2 and 3, he consistently turned in drafts late, incomplete, or not at all. As of this past Monday, which was technically the third major paper's official due date, we were meeting to discuss a draft that was barely half the required length and which, crucially, did not have an argument that responded to a problem. Creating effective arguments is probably the most important writing lesson taught in our course, and one I have been trying to teach since the first paper. Other aspects of his class work have also showed evidence of taking shortcuts, such as the class presentation. As is evidenced by the fact that we are here, I don't believe that Eric really understands why his actions were wrong, nor does he realize that he has missed out on learning how to improve his writing by working hard in this class.

## I. PRE-CASE DISCUSSION PROBLEMS SETS

Complete the chart after reading the case.

| | |
|---|---|
| Facts | |
| Opinions | |
| Assumptions | |
| Theories referred or connected to (if any) | |
| Ambiguous language | |
| Criteria you used in analyzing the case (e.g., emotional vs. rational) | |
| Emerging options | |

Write a pre-case discussion decision paper. Include these points:

a. options for case resolution

b. criteria (a rational decision should always be made with a set of criteria)

c. analysis of options

d. recommendation (of the best choice among the options)

e. action plan

## II. Case Discussion Questions

### Big-Picture Analysis

Describe the context of the case.

- institutional setting
- academic policies
- stakeholders and parties involved
- program mission and curriculum

### Stakeholders

In small groups, assume the role of one of the case stakeholders. Write a statement/ dialogue expressing this person's or group's hypothetical feelings and perspectives. Be prepared to act out your roles to the large group.

- Becky
- Linda
- Eric
- the Academic Advising Officer
- member of Academic Conduct Committee
- a colleague of Becky's in the Writing Department

### Surface Issues

What are the surface issues in this case? What is happening here from an untrained perspective? What underlying assumptions or beliefs feed into this perspective?

### Deep Issues

Discuss the real issues in the case. Try to categorize them in terms of language teaching curriculum and instruction.

### *Evidence-Based Solutions*

In groups, develop evidence-based solutions for each deep issue listed. Whenever possible, refer to a theory or principle of language learning and teaching to support your proposed solutions.

### *Teacher Thinking*

In what ways does this case influence and/or reinforce your beliefs and dispositions as a teacher? Consult the Further Resources section to help with theoretically informed solutions.

## III. POST-CASE PROBLEM SETS

### *Post-Case Analysis*

A. Categorize what you learned as:

- teacher knowledge and praxis (e.g., content knowledge, curricular knowledge, pedagogical content knowledge and application)
- teacher thinking (e.g., beliefs, problem-solving strategies, prioritizing objectives, values, professional ethics, attitudes)

B. List:

- learning objectives that you discovered in the case
- potential learning outcomes
- implications for your pedagogical practices

C. The post-case problem sets introduce reactions from various perspectives. These quotes are from others who have read the cases for educational and pedagogical purposes. Read all of the quotes and then choose two about which to write a short response (put the quotes at the top of each response).  Use these questions as a guide:

- What is the message the speaker is trying to convey? If possible, also explain why you chose the quote.
- What examples can you think of that connect to the themes presented?
- Can you relate the quote to a class discussion or to something you have read or experienced?

Quotes

1. "In my opinion, the instructor's suspicions of cheating were justified. When comparing the writing style of the self-assessment and the paper, I found the difference striking. In this earlier assignment, Eric had used much simpler vocabulary and sentences. His self-assessment also had a range of characteristic ESL grammar errors that I did not see to that extent in the draft, not to mention the paper. I was surprised by the sophisticated sentence structure and complex vocabulary in that version. Still, I am not sure if Becky could have done anything to prevent the violation."

2. "I wonder if Becky started out by doing a Google search for some of the sentences in Eric's draft. I did and could not find any online source for his paper. I wonder if another way to go about borderline cases like this one is to do a computer search on particularly sophisticated phrasing in both the student's original paper and the suspected heavily edited/rewritten version. Lack of overlap might make a stronger case for cheating, at least in the eyes of an Academic Conduct committee (which was quite lenient here). But what overworked writing teacher has time for that kind of investigation?!"

3. "From an administrative perspective (I happen to be both an administrator and a writing teacher myself), I think Becky did everything possible to give the student the benefit of the doubt and turn the incident into a teaching opportunity. She communicated repeatedly with the student and gave him multiple chances to redeem himself. The fact that he avoided communication as much as possible and stubbornly refused to see the implications proves that it was a lost cause. Like Linda, I would stand wholly behind Becky but maybe do more negotiating with the Advising office behind the scenes to facilitate the process. This case seems to show that we are limited in what we can achieve instructionally."

4. "Becky should have met with the student right away and confronted him with the discrepancy between the writing pieces. For example, she might have asked him to paraphrase some of the sophisticated passages in the paper or asked for the meaning of an especially apt word. I understand that she cared about following procedure, but I feel she should have spent more time figuring out why the student resorted to excessive outside help."

5. "I have larger questions about the drafting process involved in this case. I am curious how much time and attention are typically allocated to language issues, meaning local issues, in EAP writing classes. I've heard there are continuing debates about prioritizing work on content over language, but I am not sure what the advisable balance is. It reminds me of the artificial division between meaning and form in general ESL. And, if the teacher does not spend time working with the student on language issues, who would? Is there a support unit that does that – like a writing center with tutors?"

D. Write a reflection describing a take-away from the case in terms of praxis. Make sure to develop an action plan to resolve the case. Consider these questions as guidelines:

- In what ways did the case discussion influence your thinking about the case?
- Did you change your original decision or did the discussion reaffirm your position?
- What points had you not considered prior to the case discussion?
- How might the information you gained from this case be applicable to your current instructional setting and/or future instructional settings?
- What did you learn?
- What are you inspired to learn more about?
- How did the themes discussed in class apply to your experience?

E. Discuss what theoretical basis there is for:

- the stakeholders' behavior in the case.
- the solutions you proposed.

## Further Reading and Resources

Biber, D. (2008). *Variations across speech and writing*. Cambridge, England: Cambridge University Press.

Carlock, J., Eberhardt, M., Horst, J., & Menasche, M. (2018). *The ESL writer's handbook* (2nd ed.). Ann Arbor: University of Michigan Press.

Casanave, C.P. (2017). *Controversies in second language writing instruction: Dilemmas and decisions in research and instruction* (Second Ed.). Ann Arbor: University of Michigan Press.

Ferris, D., & Hedgcock, J. (2005). *Teaching ESL composition: Purpose, process, and practice* (2nd ed.). Mahwah, NJ: Lawrence Erlbaum.

Harris, R. (2001). *The plagiarism handbook: Strategies for preventing, detecting, and dealing with plagiarism.* Los Angeles: Pyrczak.

Marsh, B. (2007). *Plagiarism: Alchemy and remedy in higher education.* Albany: State University of New York Press.

Mott-Smith, J.A., Tomaš, Z., & Kostka, I. (2017). *Teaching effective source use: Classroom approaches that work.* Ann Arbor: University of Michigan Press.

Paterson, K., with Wedge, R. (2013). *Oxford grammar for EAP: English grammar and practice for academic Purposes.* Oxford, England: Oxford University Press.

Purdue University Online Writing Lab (OWL). Retrieved from http://owl.english.purdue.edu

Turabian, K. (2010). *Student's guide to writing college papers.* Chicago: University of Chicago Press.

Whitley, B.E., & Keith-Spiegel, P. (2002). *Academic dishonesty: An educator's guide.* Mahwah, NJ: Lawrence Erlbaum.

# ▪▪▪▪▪▪▪▪▪▪▪▪▪▪▪▪ CASE 5.3 ▪▪▪▪▪▪▪▪▪▪▪▪▪▪▪▪
# Lakeborough College

Students walk in—some nonchalantly, some rushed, their umbrellas dripping and steaming—and then spread out in different corners of the third-floor classroom that can house about 20 students. It's a small seminar class with modern movable desks in one of the coziest buildings on campus. Perched on the front desk/lectern is Ms. Oliver, who greets everyone, occasionally venturing a "how are you today" that few students respond to. The agenda is already on the board, with a list of the homework.

Twelve students are now more or less settled in. By the looks of it, the class has a dream ESL makeup: a good gender mix, one-third Asian, a few Caucasian faces, and a couple of Middle Easterners.

Ms. Oliver announces: "Here's what we'll cover today. The essay on gender roles, argument structure, templates on nominalization, and academic vocabulary. I have several handouts for you. Please pass them around."

The pile of notes is going around the room, students whispering while counting out the three separate topics.

"So what did you think of the essay 'The Forgotten Ladies'?"

Two girls giggle. A young man looks up and mumbles: "Kind of interesting, but is that the real situation that they describe?"

Ms. Oliver looks at the student who spoke up and asks, "What do they describe?"

"Well, how some women in China don't get married and how society looks at them. But is that for real?"

One of the Asian girls says, "We don't know the percentages, but there are a lot of young women who are well educated and cannot find husbands."

Another chimes in: "Or decide not to marry at all."

"They are probably ugly!" adds Diego, who hails from Brazil.

"They don't make the decision to marry or not. It's the father who decides," says Amir.

"No, it's not," a determined chorus of Asian girls adds.

"Of course it is—right, Arwa?" Amir turns to the girl in head cover.

Arwa looks up from her open book and says to the professor, avoiding Amir: "It depends on the family, really. My father would care about what I think."

"But he will make the decision—we are not China," Amir states.

"Things are changing, no? Young people in any country now take charge of their lives, I think." This is from Valentina.

Arwa looks quizzically at Ms. Oliver, who is focused on the textbook. "Let's look at the structure of the essay and what data the author provides," she says. "Data matters. This is an academic essay."

The students quickly point out the statistics quoted in the text, and a sense of resignation seems to set in.

"What else makes the essay academic? Look at the text and find features of academic style," she says.

The students cluster in what seem like practiced groups—the girls on one side and boys on the other—and start parsing the essay.

"Are we looking for vocabulary?" asks Amir.

"No, the structure of the text," replies Valentina.

"Or both?" wonders Pavel.

Ms. Oliver walks around, points at the handouts she distributed, and says, "Look at nominalizations. Can you count them in the text?"

The students shuffle papers, searching for the right handout to match patterns.

Diego claims he found one, but he is not quite sure. Yun raises her hand for another one.

"So, what is the template you are following?" Ms. Oliver rallies the tentative troops. "N+N (+N), right? Why are they using it?"

No one looks up, and she continues almost immediately: "It helps pack information more concisely. It's useful in science writing, when you have to describe concepts or phenomena by compiling their characteristics without repeating the definition over and over," she explains.

"What about specific vocabulary? Do you see any terms that you can associate with the topic of the essay and also use outside it? *Socioeconomic? Demographic trend? Social expectations?* For homework, find more and make a list. Now let's move on to argumentation. Pull up the handout on rhetorical patterns."

The class is now configured in random groups with the task of discussing how writing is typically organized in various cultures. The students seem engaged and the room is abuzz for the next five minutes.

Ms. Oliver then starts packing her things, and the class is dismissed. Before she can get to the door, three students have lined up at her desk. They have questions about various points in the class and about the homework. Ms. Oliver ruffles through the pile of handouts and points to potential answers: "Read that definition. You have to work independently, you're in college now. And I can't answer emails about all kinds of things that you were supposed to get in class. By the way, your email style is sometimes inappropriate: too informal or too direct. You have to be careful not to make a bad first impression!"

The students look at each other sheepishly, wondering who is at fault. They linger in the classroom, poring over the handouts well after Ms. Oliver has left.

## ■ Exhibit A: Institutional Overview

This class is part of the preparatory academic program of a liberal arts research college. The goals of the course are characteristic of EAP courses:

- Read academic texts on varied subjects with accurate comprehension and intellectual discernment.
- Recognize and use the conventions of expository and argumentative discourse.
- Develop the tools to critique academic texts in a balanced manner.
- Express oneself with linguistic accuracy, fluency, and diction appropriate to a university environment.
- Understand U.S. academic conventions.
- Develop self-monitoring strategies for academic communication.

The course sections, capped at 15 students, typically consist of well-educated, intellectually disposed international students from diverse ethnic and linguistic backgrounds. The small seminar format allows students to participate actively and to get appropriate attention and feedback from the instructor. At the completion of the course, the students are expected to be acculturated to academia and to possess the skills and competences that allow them to function effectively as students in the disciplines of their choice.

### ▌ Exhibit B: Rhetorical Patterns across Language Groups (Class Handout)

*Thought Patterns*

Perhaps, you have never considered this before, but the way you develop ideas may be determined by your native language and culture. Being fluent in a second language means more than just learning the words of the language: You must also learn its thought patterns.

*Asian languages*

The topic being discussed is never directly attacked; it is discussed in terms of what it is not, rather than what it is. One point of view is not adopted; the topic is viewed from many different perspectives.

*Romance languages*

Here, the topic is addressed, but there is more freedom to digress, as long as eventually the topic is once again discussed. Sentences resulting from this thought pattern tend to be longer than sentences in English.

*Semitic languages*

The topic is addressed through a series of parallel ideas, where information is added, or additional information is the opposite of the original information. More coordinating conjunctions are used than in English, where those do not usually indicate sophisticated thought processes.

*Germanic languages (English is one of these)*

The topic is addressed directly. All information about the topic must directly relate to it, and leads in a straight line to a conclusion. Sophistication of thought is marked by the use of subordinating conjunctions. Reasoning in English can be inductive or deductive (in most cases).

*Discussion*

Consider your first language. What are indications of sophisticated thought, or of good writing, in it? How do they differ from English?

## ▮ Exhibit C: Nominalizations (Class Handout)

Nominalizations are noun structures formed from a different word class or a clause. Nominalizations are frequently used in academic writing, as they are able to pack a lot of information in a condensed form. Most of the meaning in expository writing can be expressed through noun phrases, but beware of overusing them: They can make your style too dense and hard to process.

1. <u>Nominalization patterns</u> (based on corpus analysis of noun phrases)
**Determiner+ (premodifier)+ head noun+ (postmodifier)** (…) = optional element

Examples: our (discussion) team of (students)
the (changing socioeconomic) situation (for mid-career) professionals

2. Now, search for at least five other examples of nominalizations in the essay and list them here (with corresponding page numbers):

**Homework**: Unpack the nominalizations you found by expressing the same meaning through other structures.

Ex: A marriage certificate was a passport into adulthood → When you married you were considered an adult.

<u>Note</u>: Keep in mind that, in some cases, using a nominalization is the most effective way to express the desired meaning (ex: The region strives to create *First World health-care and retirement systems for people of different income levels.*), and a paraphrase will result in a convoluted sentence. If you found such examples in the text, please list them separately.

■ **Exhibit D: Discussion Phrases (Class Handout)**

*The following structures, categorized thematically, will help you communicate in academic situations.*

Responding to a question

*That's a good question.*
*That's an interesting question.*
*That's a difficult question.*
*That's a complex question.*
*I'm sorry. I didn't understand the question. Can you repeat it?*

Politely Disagreeing

*Well, I don't necessarily agree with that.*
*I see it somewhat differently.*
*I wouldn't say that.*
*However, it can equally be argued that...*

Politely Disagreeing (Hedging)

*I see what you mean/your point, but...*
*That may be true, but...*
*Yes, but on the other hand...*
*Well, maybe so, but...*
*Yes, I agree, but...*
*That's a very good point, but…*
*Perhaps, but don't you think that...*
*I'm pretty much in agreement with you, but…*
*But wouldn't you agree that...*

Asking someone else to contribute

*X, what do you think?*
*X, would you like to add something to that?*
*X, you look like you want to say something.*

Polite questions

*Do you mind if I ask you what/why/when/... ?*
*Would you mind telling me whether...?*
*I'd like to find out...*

Helping the audience understand

*X, did I make myself clear?; Does this answer your question?*

## I. PRE-CASE DISCUSSION PROBLEMS SETS

Complete the chart after reading the case.

| Facts | |
|---|---|
| Opinions | |
| Assumptions | |
| Theories referred or connected to (if any) | |
| Ambiguous language | |
| Criteria you used in analyzing the case (e.g., emotional vs. rational) | |
| Emerging options | |

Write a pre-case discussion decision paper. Include these points:

a. options for case resolution

b. criteria (a rational decision should always be made with a set of criteria)

c. analysis of options

d. recommendation (of the best choice among the options)

e. action plan

## II. CASE DISCUSSION QUESTIONS

### Big-Picture Analysis

Describe the context of the case.

- institutional setting
- student demographics and needs
- curricular field
- teacher professional profile (relevant skills and knowledge)

### Stakeholders

In small groups, assume the role of one of the case stakeholders. Write a statement/dialogue expressing this person's or group's hypothetical feelings and perspectives. Be prepared to act out your roles to the large group.

- Ms. Oliver
- Yun
- Amir
- Arwa
- the rest of the students in the class
- an EAP colleague visiting the class

### Surface Issues

What are the surface issues in this case? What is happening here from an untrained perspective? What underlying assumptions or beliefs feed into this perspective?

### Deep Issues

Discuss the real issues in the case. Try to categorize them in terms of language teaching curriculum and instruction.

## *Evidence-Based Solutions*

In groups, develop evidence-based solutions for each deep issue listed. Whenever possible, refer to a theory or principle of language learning and teaching to support your proposed solutions.

## *Teacher Thinking*

In what ways does this case influence and/or reinforce your beliefs and dispositions as a teacher? Consult the Further Resources section to help with theoretically informed solutions.

# III. POST-CASE PROBLEM SETS

## *Post-Case Analysis*

A. Categorize what you learned as:
- teacher knowledge and praxis (e.g., content knowledge, curricular knowledge, pedagogical content knowledge and application)
- teacher thinking (e.g., beliefs, problem-solving strategies, prioritizing objectives, values, professional ethics, attitudes)

B. List:
- learning objectives that you discovered in the case
- potential learning outcomes
- implications for your pedagogical practices

C. The post-case problem sets introduce reactions from various perspectives. These quotes are from others who have read the cases for educational and pedagogical purposes. Read all of the quotes and then choose two about which to write a short response (put the quotes at the top of each response). Use these questions as a guide:
- What is the message the speaker is trying to convey? If possible, also explain why you chose the quote.
- What examples can you think of that connect to the themes presented?
- Can you relate the quote to a class discussion or to something you have read or experienced?

Quotes

1. "I was shocked by how hands-off Ms. Oliver was. She was obviously experienced and knowledgeable, so I wonder if the expectation for student independence in handling the various tasks is a standard feature of EAP—maybe as part of building academic literacy?"

2. "The cross-cultural dynamic in this class is fascinating to watch. There is a clear power game based on traditional gender roles, but the teacher never takes a position or encourages any of the students to comment on the conflicting positions expressed by Amir and Arwa. Some suggestions: She should step in and use the essay they read, but barely discussed, as a basis for a broader discussion about the expectations of women in some traditional communities. She could even organize a mini-debate on that, or even better, an informal poll on the issue across the class. This would in fact validate her own claim that data matter in EAP!"

3. "The teacher seemed to have prepared for the class, but she did not really teach it. She did not explain the handouts or follow-up on any of the questions that the students ventured. There seemed to be uneasiness in the class that she did not try to address or dispel. I think she did care about the students' learning, but did not help the students in building any study skills."

4. "I am curious about the content aspect of the class. In EAP, modeling academic discourse is a primary goal. Still, Ms. Oliver did little of that; in fact, she was herself a bad model of academic interaction."

5. "The lesson plan and choice of materials concern me: the teacher tried to integrate a full essay, a discussion of structure, vocabulary, and even some grammar. The transition from task to task and material to material was confusing, though. Also, what criteria did Ms. Oliver use to elicit the academic vocabulary from the essay? It seems the class was discussing a social science text, but she did not provide any guidance about the key concepts to take away and apply across the discipline."

D. Write a reflection describing a take-away from the case in terms of praxis. Make sure to develop an action plan to resolve the case. Consider these questions as guidelines:

- In what ways did the case discussion influence your thinking about the case?
- Did you change your original decision or did the discussion reaffirm your position?
- What points had you not considered prior to the case discussion?
- How might the information you gained from this case be applicable to your current instructional setting and/or future instructional settings?
- What did you learn?
- What are you inspired to learn more about?
- How did the themes discussed in class apply to your experience?

E. Discuss what theoretical basis there is for:

- the stakeholders' behavior in the case.
- the solutions you proposed.

## Further Reading and Resources

Biber, D. (2006). *University language: A corpus-based study of spoken and written registers.* Amsterdam: John Benjamins.

Brown, P., & Levinson, S. (1987). *Politeness: Some universals in language usage.* Cambridge, England: Cambridge University Press.

Byram, M., & Feng, A. (2004). Culture and language learning: teaching, research and scholarship. *Language Teaching, 37,* 149–168.

Grabe, W. (2009). *Reading in a second language: Moving from theory to practice.* Cambridge, England: Cambridge University Press.

Harbon, L. (2013). Second language teachers and intercultural literacy. *International Journal of Innovation in English Language Teaching Research, 2*(1), 77–78.

Hyland, K. (2006). *English for academic purposes: An advanced resource book.* Abingdon, England: Routledge.

Kaplan, R. (1966). Cultural thought patterns in intercultural education. *Language Learning, 16*(1), 1–20.

Kostogriz, A., & Tsolidis, G. (2008). Transcultural literacy: Between the global and the local. *Pedagogy, Culture and Society, 16,* 125–136.

Liu, J., Chang, Y., Yang, F., & Sun, Y. (2011). "Is what I need what I want?" Reconceptualizing college students' needs in English courses for general and specific/academic purposes. *Journal of English for Academic Purposes, 10*, 271–280.

Matsuda, P.K., & DePew, K.E. (2002). Early second language writing: An introduction. *Journal of Second Language Writing, 11*, 261–268.

Moran, P.R. (2001). *Teaching culture: Perspectives in practice.* Boston: Heinle & Heinle.

Swales, J. (2004). *Research genres: Explorations and applications.* New York: Cambridge University Press.

# Chapter 6

# Applications

In our dynamic, globalized world, language learning has become a means to cross linguistic and cultural boundaries and to support integration and academic literacy to ensure equitable education opportunities and social justice. The 21$^{st}$ century language teacher's competencies should integrate a solid theoretical and pedagogical base along with cultural responsiveness, open-mindedness, contextual flexibility, and problem-solving orientations. With its emphasis on reflective practice and validating learners' experiences, case-based pedagogy is particularly attuned to the needs of language educators. It is designed to promote teachers' critical thinking by asking them to distinguish between facts and assumptions and surface and deep issues, as well as to critically analyze contextual factors and multiple perspectives to co-construct evidence-based solutions. Case-based pedagogy guides its practitioners toward creative, yet grounded, solutions to common issues in contemporary language classrooms, while simultaneously providing the lifelong professional value of collaboration in the field of language teaching and learning.

The distinguishing feature of this book is that it allows practitioners to read, analyze, and debate reflectively about carefully selected cases from authentic learning and teaching contexts that represent typical challenges. It provides current and aspiring language educators with the opportunity to develop an evidence-based, structured approach to thinking about and solving practical dilemmas.

The overarching themes that run through the cases include: student motivation factors and language acquisition; integrated skills and task-based language instruction; contextualized and content-based language teaching; cooperative and communicative teaching and learning techniques; culturally sensitive pedagogy and differentiated instruction; standards-based and varied lesson design and assessment; reflective practice and flexible thinking; collaborative problem-solving and teamwork; and administrative engagement and oversight. Even though this is not a finite list, it showcases the transformative potential of the case-based methodology in that it sensitizes practitioners to become acute observers and hones their ability to assess emerging challenges and develop an effective plan of action.

Among the many advantages of this case-based approach are: It is scalable and can be adapted to various educational settings; it reflects the complexity of the modern language learning classroom; it is attuned to the learning styles and needs of global citizens; it is engaging, empowering, and professionally rewarding for both the case facilitators and the participants; it offers a productive blend of theory and practice; and it is inclusive, yet personalized, and meaningful.

A possible extension of the method could be to assign the writing of the cases to the participants. We have occasionally used that format with participants who have more advanced formal training and teaching experience. By harnessing the experiences of pre-service and in-service language teachers, cases generated by them could augment the scope of the issues under scrutiny and satisfy the learners' need for immediate application of knowledge. If that option were chosen, the outline that follows provides guidance to case writing.

## Guide to Writing a Case

### Step One: *Reflect and Write*

In a one-page journal reflection, describe in detail what you perceive to be one of the most significant instructional, professional, or programmatic dilemmas that you have experienced when teaching language learners.

## Step Two: *Outline Key Concepts*

A well-written case must include a detailed explanation of these elements, which are usually presented in the form of "exhibits":

| Topic | Details |
|---|---|
| The school context (mission statements, demographic information, sociocultural setting, etc.) | |
| The instructional program (curricular excerpts, program descriptions, or other relevant information about the curricular and learning environment) | |
| The classroom (classroom settings from physical environment to affective aspects of the setting, such as teachers' and students' attitudes) | |
| The characters (rich description of the key characters' backgrounds and quotes/conversations/discourse that describe the dilemma) | |
| The dilemma (plot of the situation) | |

## Step 3: *Drafting*

Use the outline to guide your first draft writing of the case. The case should be written in the third person and should tell a story. You may include quotations from characters in the case, school mission statements, references to standards, or whatever you think will provide a comprehensive picture of the complexity of the issue. As a writer of the case, your view should be neutral; the case should have no assumptions, stated conclusions, or arguments. However, since these student case studies will be used for in-class case method discussions, it is important that you provide sufficient information upon which your colleagues will be able to base their arguments and conclusions when analyzing your case. For the purposes of professional confidentiality, it is important *not* to provide the real names of the subjects or school involved, so you need to substitute the real names with imaginary ones.

## Step 4: *Peer Editing*

Exchange your case with a partner in class. Read his/her case and complete this rubric to discuss first draft strengths and areas in need of improvement.

---

**Peer Editing Checklist**

---

1.  Is the case written in third person and does it tell a story?          Y/N

2.  Does the case include authentic information for analysis?          Y/N
    (e.g., quotations from characters in the case, school mission
    statements, references to standards, or whatever you think will
    provide a comprehensive picture of the complexity of the issue.)

3.  Is the author's view neutral? Does the case have no stated          Y/N
    conclusions or arguments?

4.  Does the case provide enough information in all categories to          Y/N
    analyze in a class discussion?

5.  Does the case present a relevant and meaningful topic for class          Y/N
    discussion?

6.  What are the case draft's strengths and weaknesses?

## Step 5: *Revise*

Taking your peer's feedback into consideration, revise and edit a final draft of your case study.

The additional resources and online Commentary should also ensure a productive case discussion and set a model for successful future application of the case methodology. We wish you enjoyable and rewarding teacher training.